Start Everything Finish Nothing

The Man Who Moved The Army-Navy Game

Lessons learned from multiple careers that will get you from start to finish.
How to get it done!

Rolfe G. Arnhym

Publisher
Digalign, LLC
1228 E 7th Ave Ste 200
Tampa, FL 33605
For further information please visit www.rolfegarnhym.com

Start Everything Finish Nothing
©2014 Rolfe G. Arnhym
ISBN, print ed. 978-0-9909798-0-7 (Paperback)
ISBN, print ed. 978-0-9909798-1-4 (Hardback)
ISBN, electronic book text 978-0-9909798-2-1 (Mobi)
ISBN, electronic book text 978-0-9909798-3-8 (EPUB)

Cover Design: Derek Sell
Photos by: Ryan Gautier

First Printing: 2014

Dedication

To my wife, June, for her love, patience, and unwavering support as we lived the experiences that led to never ending lessons learned.

To our daughters, Kathy (Husband Fitz Conner, Grandsons Jamie and Reid. and Granddaughter Kristen) and Carolyn (Husband John Johnson, Grandson Daniel, and Granddaughter Jennifer), for their unquestionable love and encouragement.

To my Vistage Associates, who not only urged me to "start" and "finish" this book, but who also inadvertently provided me with even more situations that gave substance and clarity to the need for the chapters that lie ahead of you.

To the US Military Academy at West Point, for molding me and giving me a compass that has guided me through multiple careers following over 20 years as an Infantry Officer.

Finally, to those of you that will read this book - learn from it and carry the torch!

Acknowledgements

I would like to thank Barry Powers, Floyd Kemske, Hannah Hubner, Derek Sell, and the entire team at Digalign for their work on this book. Without them, this would have been something to add to my "start everything, finish nothing" pile. We all know how much I would have hated that.

Table of Contents

Prologue

A Massive Peacetime Troop Movement

Yogi Berra once said, "When you come to a fork in the road, take it."

He was giving directions to Joe Garagiola for reaching his home in New Jersey, but the aphorism is a profound meditation on time management. On any given day, you face a fork in the road - one branch looks clear, the other has an obstacle. You look at the obstacle and decide, "All right, I'm going to take a break here, and I'm going to do something that perhaps is a little bit easier that will give me some satisfaction of having accomplished something today." You promise yourself you will return to the fork and look at the other branch tomorrow.

You started your work with good intentions, but something got in the way. It doesn't make a great deal of difference what that obstacle is. It could be you just don't have enough time to get the job done and you put it off to another day. It could be that you just don't know what to do next or how to do it. You could lack resources, financial or material. You may have the wrong people. All of these are potential obstacles to keep you from going forward.

But if you've ever served in the Army, you're familiar with the obstacle course, where failure, as they say, is not an option. You've got to overcome each obstacle and move on to the next one. Nothing gives you greater satisfaction than being able to take down the obstacles one at a time until you're finally finished and you've accomplished what you set out to do, which in this case is finish the obstacle course.

We all view obstacles differently. The question is do we have the strength of mind and body to overcome them and to move on - or are we going to take the fork in the road? If you take the fork every time, you will find that you are starting everything and finishing nothing. You may have small satisfactions in your day-to-day life, but you'll never experience the deep and abiding fulfillment of finishing the obstacle course.

I have worked my way through my share of obstacles in my life, but the one that looms largest in my memory was the one that resulted in what can only be described as a massive peacetime troop movement. I am talking about moving the Army-Navy game from Philadelphia to Pasadena in November of 1983. I'm going to tell you that story because I think each obstacle – and there were many – appeared insurmountable. But every time one of these obstacles arose, I ignored the voice that told me to take the fork in the road and engaged the obstacle. It was a great life lesson for me. I hope it is for you, too.

When Failure Is Not an Option
Look at the obstacles you have faced in life. When you were a child, someone told you, "No." When you got to school, you had to do homework and take tests. Then, for some of us, each grade of school was an obstacle, and then

came middle school, then high school, and finally college. With obstacles like these, no wonder they put a cap and gown on you and played Pomp and Circumstance every time you completed one. Finally, you faced the obstacle of getting your first job, and you learned what it is to engage an obstacle that your best efforts might not overcome because somebody else was deciding the outcome.

Here's an obstacle of a different character. I served two one-year tours in combat in South Vietnam. Combat is like the obstacle course. Failure is not an option. You must make a decision and move forward. You have two imperatives: you need to win and you need to take care of your men. The only way to get through it is to treat each obstacle as an opportunity.

The lesson I learned in South Vietnam was the one I most often applied in moving the Army-Navy game to Pasadena.

At the time, I was the CEO of the Pasadena Chamber of Commerce. My mission was to improve the business climate and opportunities for business growth. The Army-Navy game project started in 1981, while I was watching the Army-Navy game on TV in my family room in California with my wife and a few friends, it occurred to me that the game should move around the country. After all, the military academies belong to the nation. In addition, Philadelphia as a community seemed largely indifferent to the game being played there, and attendance and revenue had been going down.

When I looked into it, I learned that west of the Mississippi, recruiting for both Cadets and Midshipmen was slow. Bringing the game to Pasadena could help with the recruiting problem, as it could serve as a pilot project for moving the game around the country the way I thought it should move. It could also mean a lot for the business climate and business growth in Pasadena.

I tried out my idea of moving the game to Pasadena on the nearest person: my wife. She said it couldn't be done. I shared the idea with other people. They said it couldn't be done. Such red flags deter normal people, I guess, but I've always regarded a red flag the way a bull regards a red cape – as a signal to charge.

I realized that some of my initial obstacles were going to be people. The Board of my Chamber of Commerce, the City Council in Pasadena, not to mention the Secretary of Defense, the Secretary of Army, the Secretary of the Navy, the Superintendents of the respective academies and their staffs, the Athletic Directors – all of these had to be convinced that this was a good idea.

At West Point, Cadets run a celebrated indoor obstacle course that poses 11 obstacles to completion. The first one is a low-crawl of about 20 feet, where you crawl on all fours as fast you can under a barrier of regularly spaced horizontal boards. The first time you face this obstacle, it looks somewhat daunting. The thing to remember is that each step of your crawl is about a foot, and the only thing in your way when you start is the first step of your crawl. Then you face the next step, and the next, and so on. The point is that even the most imposing obstacle can be reduced to many small obstacles. If you just keep on overcoming the small obstacles, you will complete it.

Knowing that I had a large population to convince, I decided to begin with the first step and start making calls and visiting with key decision makers in Pasadena. By and large, I found that everybody liked the concept but they looked at me rather quizzically and said, "You know there are just too many obstacles here. You're going to have to find a way to move Cadets and Midshipmen across the country. You're going to have to figure out how you're going to feed and house them. Where are you going to put them? Where's the money going to come from?" Most importantly, everyone was concerned about at some level being exposed either financially or put at risk if it did not work. Many just thought it was a lousy idea, while most were simply overwhelmed by the enormity of the task.

That led me to my next obstacle: building an organization. I would need team members, I would need to identify leaders, and most important of all, we would need to assemble an enormous amount of money. I took it breakfast-by-breakfast, lunch-by-lunch, meeting after meeting, phone call after phone call, letter after letter. Eventually, interest began to build in the idea of moving the Army-Navy game from Philadelphia to the Rose Bowl in Pasadena.

Having built interest in Pasadena, I was ready to move on to the next, and much more difficult obstacle: I had to convince the academies. I set up a dialogue with the Athletic Directors, the Commandant of Cadets, and the Commandant of the Midshipmen, and the respective Superintendents of the two academies to determine their willingness to see the game moved from Philadelphia to the Rose Bowl. Probably a big factor in the case of the Athletic Directors and the staff and key leaders within the two academies was the fact that attendance had been declining over the last few years in Philadelphia. This, of course, translates into a revenue loss for the two athletic programs - a key element in any decision is defining the need.

Aided by Philadelphia's Complacency

Then there was the City of Philadelphia. In one sense, Philadelphia was my ally - it had become complacent about hosting the game. Philadelphia is halfway between the two Academies and had hosted the game for nearly every year since 1890 (except for the travel-restricted years of World War II), on the Saturday after Thanksgiving. In the 1970s and 1980s, the people of Philadelphia were generally aware the game was being held, but it did not have the level of support and interest that would reflect the true energy of the host city. Granted, there were a number of people within the City of Philadelphia who saw this as the event of the year, and their efforts have to be applauded. But generally, it was just another event on the Saturday after Thanksgiving, and attendance on the part of folks from the Philadelphia area was falling. Of course, this was exacerbated by the fact that the Academies' football seasons had not looked all that good for a couple of years.

Still, it was America's game and a major tradition - a spark was missing and something clearly had to be done. Obviously, from my seat in Pasadena, California I was not in a position to ignite fires in Philadelphia. What I could do, however, was to get their attention by proposing that the game move. In July of 1982, I wrote a letter to the Secretary of the Army and to the Secretary of the Navy. In that letter, I specifically proposed that the 1983 Army-Navy game be played in Pasadena's 106,000-seat Rose Bowl. I noted that we had been in contact with the Athletic Directors at West Point and Annapolis, as well as officials in the Department of Defense, Department of the Air Force, and the White House staff.

While we did not have direct personal contact with the Service Secretaries, I was very, very fortunate to have established a personal relationship with the Secretary of the Air Force, who was a native of Pasadena and who opened the necessary doors. A very important lesson here is the importance and the value of relationships and relationship building. My partner in all of this was Bob Finch, the Lieutenant Governor under then-Governor Reagan, and through him I was able to get introductions to the Secretary of Defense, Casper Weinberger, and to a number of key officials in the White House. Opening doors, which are obstacles unto themselves, is no easy task but admittedly, but as you build on relationships these doors open one by one; at least we had an opportunity to make our case known.

Here are some of the points we made in our proposal:

- The Athletic Departments at the two academies were not getting the sort of revenue that they should be getting from the game.
- Recruiting and admission efforts in the western half of the United States for the respective academies had slowed.
- The largest active and retired military population was located in California first and Texas second.
- Moving the game to the Rose Bowl would be an enormous boost for the program in terms of potential attendance and media attention.
- Finally, moving the game would be an enormous public affairs win via direct Cadet/Midshipmen

interaction with the population with the Los Angeles area.

Frankly, this was a sales pitch. If you've ever done any selling, you know the single most important success factor is in how well you focus on the needs of the customer. Accordingly, we had to focus on the needs of the academies, not the needs of Pasadena. Besides, Pasadena's needs were covered implicitly. We were looking at another football game in the Rose Bowl, with considerable associated revenue and obviously, the prestige of having held and conducted the Army-Navy game in our city, so it would be a win-win for both sides. A win for Pasadena because it meant substantial support for the Chamber of Commerce; a win for West Point and Annapolis because of improved attendance and revenue at the Army-Navy game itself. Generating greater interest west of the Mississippi on the part of potential Cadets and Midshipmen was also a win as you will learn later – it worked!

A Massive Troop Movement

Obviously, the need to move almost 10,000 Cadets and Midshipmen across the country and back at no expense to the academies was a bit of a challenge. Needless to say housing and feeding some 10,000 Cadets and Midshipmen, along with moving them about the city of Los Angeles for events and activities represented major obstacles that had to be overcome. There was still one other obstacle and that was that the one-year escape clause in the contract with Philadelphia had escaped, making it was too late to move the game without breaking the contract. We made a proposal to Philadelphia to extend its contract for two years, provided it would allow a one-year absence.

If we couldn't get Philadelphia to agree, we would have to wait until 1985, when the current contract expired. By virtue of multiple negotiations at every level, we overcame this obstacle and the City of Philadelphia graciously agreed to the contract extension, which allowed a one-year escape clause and that escape was to take place in the fall of 1983, specifically the first Saturday in December. While we waited for a decision, we put together a budget, which estimated that the cost of the move would be approximately $6 million. Our team also began to look at how we were going to house and feed the Cadets and Midshipmen. All of this would need to happen with the timing and precision of a close-order drill, for the Academies would not consider the possibility of missed classes.

While waiting for decisions from the Academies, from the Secretary of Defense, and the Secretaries of Army and Navy, we built our team and created an organizational structure that almost looked like the invasion of Normandy. I already had an administrative assistant on board, but I also had to put some other people in place. They included people responsible for plans and operations, public relations, and media. We had to anticipate TV, housing, data processing, transportation, special events, fundraising, game management, security, and traffic control. We needed to identify hotels to house the cadets and Midshipmen, a host committee to deal with the Cadets and Midshipmen themselves, plans for ground movement, plans for air movement, and folks in charge of protocol, corporate relations, and memorabilia.

In other words, there was a great deal to be accomplished. As the summer of 1982 came to a close, we were acutely aware that every passing day brought us closer to the first

Saturday in December 1983 and reduced the amount of time we had to work with.

It wasn't just a football game. There would also be a series of events and activities that would take place while the Cadets and Midshipmen were in Pasadena, which included a special event utilizing the combined glee clubs to honor Bob Hope and a TV special that came out of that. A band review, which included the bands from the two academies, a Mayor's breakfast, a Governor's lunch, nights at Disney, a Congressional reception, fundraising events, coaches' breakfast, and a parade into the stadium for the traditional march on ceremony were also included in the festivities. We also had to plan outreach to the greater Los Angeles area and beyond, including contacts in Hawaii, San Diego, San Francisco, Portland, and Seattle.

In October of 1982, the respective Secretaries of Defense, Army, and Navy had approved of the concept of moving the game, which added further impetus to keep us moving towards an approval. Our plan was to have all of the details in place no later than January of 1983. In February 1983, we got a little bit of a surprise: the Secretary of Navy insisted we'd have to house 1,000 Cadets and 1,000 Midshipmen in hotels. We were at a loss as to why, but were not going to break China arguing about it.

Hotel accommodations for 2,000 Cadets and Midshipmen were going to add cost. Within the Chamber of Commerce itself in Pasadena, I was being leaned on pretty heavily to utilize the various bands from the high schools in our community to house the Cadets and Midshipmen. The idea was that we would pay the bands and the band members in turn would provide housing. So at the end of the day, the cost of hotels for these 2,000 wasn't a new cost, just an increased one. The bands saw the hosting plan as a fundraiser, where we would pay a certain amount of money to each band to host and house the Cadets and Midshipmen. Whether we paid the bands or the hotels, I had to factor this into the budget. Then there was the cost of getting the rest of the Cadets and Midshipmen housed in Pasadena – another 8,000 people. I had already successfully concluded discussions with United Airlines and they had agreed to move the entire Corp of Cadets and the Brigade of Midshipmen across the country and back, utilizing their data systems. Through their computerized programs, we would be able to program the Cadets and Midshipmen literally from their rooms at West Point and Annapolis through ground transportation to their respective departure airports to Los Angeles and back again. At a little over $200 apiece, it was a very reasonable price.

Our First Big Interrupter

In February 1983, we're looking ahead with a football game to be played on the first Saturday in December, roughly nine months to complete the development of the plan, and raise some $6 million dollars plus to support it. Little did we know how optimistic *that* was!

Although we had barely enough time to pull this off, in April 1983 we were struck with our first big interrupter. That month, at the NCAA Basketball Final Four in Albuquerque (the committee that assigned games to television networks) decided to have the Army-Navy game played on the Friday after Thanksgiving. All our plans were based on the first Saturday in December, as the game had never been played before Thanksgiving before. In one stroke, that committee wiped away a week of our planning time, thrust us into the busiest travel week of the year, and dropped us into the kickoff of the holiday shopping season. What a nightmare.

Like Hannibal in the Alps, we had come too far. There was no turning back. We just had to increase our pace and march on.

United Airlines provided service into Baltimore, so when we made the decision that the Naval Academy would fly via United Airlines it simplified half the airlift. But United did not provide service to Stewart Field in Newburgh, which was the departure venue for West Point. Another interrupter. The cost to move them by ground to Newark or New York City was prohibitive.

I set about identifying a number of other carriers to move the Corp of Cadets from West Point. I can tell you that some of my classmates and some of the folks that I was dealing with were not very happy with this decision that, candidly, was sort of forced on me; I had to band together a bunch of charter airlines so that we could complete the move of the Corp of Cadets. The facts are that, with the exception of one glitch, we were able to leave on time and complete the entire move of almost 10,000 Cadets and Midshipmen across the country approximately 3,000 miles flawlessly. There was another interrupter after that: one of the carriers went into bankruptcy coincident with their planned departure from Stewart Field. I'll touch on that a little bit later.

Using charter airlines for the Cadets was going to add to the overall expense, so to save some money and the cost of paying bands to house Cadets and Midshipmen, I reached out to the sports editor for the CBS affiliate in Los Angeles to get me on TV. I'd had an idea that came to me out of the blue. I went on TV to ask the people in Los Angeles to be host families for some 8,000 Cadets and Midshipmen. (You will recall that the other 2,000 had to stay in hotels.) My pitch was simple: wouldn't you like to have a Cadet or a Midshipman in your home for the Thanksgiving holiday? I should add that I had a battle on my hands when I created the idea of band hosts.

That appeal took off like a rocket and to our complete surprise, we were hopelessly oversubscribed. To accomplish this, we literally appealed to some 31 cities in the Los Angeles area. What was an imperative is that the Midshipmen by and large were going to be landing at LAX via United Airlines. The charter airlines, and to include American Airlines, were all going to be flying into Ontario, California. In a nutshell, my problem was figuring out how to link them up with their host families without creating a complete disaster at those respective airports. I came up with a busing plan and, for a lack of another better term, "Zip Code Commanders." The "Zip Code Commanders" were stationed in various schools and shopping centers around the Los Angeles area with a mission of assembling the host families said those locations, so that we wouldn't create a disaster at either LAX or Ontario, which was on the eastern side of Los Angeles.

Obviously, the next piece was a rather sophisticated busing plan to get the Cadets and Midshipmen from the two airports out to the various neighborhoods where host families were standing by. Incredibly, the plan worked to perfection. The Cadets and Midshipmen were picked up and safely taken to various shopping centers, malls, and school parking lots, where they were matched up with host families.

I will depart briefly from this discussion to add a side note. Having a couple of Cadets and a couple Midshipmen with host families had a beautiful side effect. The relationships that were created have extended to this day, resulting in no small number of marriages, long standing relationships and friendships. It was probably one of the most rewarding aspects of the move of the Army-Navy game itself to the Rose Bowl.

I was still stuck with another problem: we had 1,000 Cadets and 1,000 Midshipmen staying in hotels in the Los Angeles area, and they had to be fed, which obviously added cost. We went back out to those families who had volunteered to host a Cadet or Midshipman that we were not able to provide them with Cadets and Midshipmen for that weekend and asked if they would like to have them for Thanksgiving dinner. Once again, that worked like a charm and we were able to provide Thanksgiving dinner for all the Cadets and all the Midshipmen. Additionally, it did not become another line item on my budget, which was gradually reaching a critical stage.

The Problem of Mascots
The obstacle that got the most public attention had to do with the Academy mascots. Needless to say, the Academies are used to having their respective mascots at the game. In the Army's case it was the Army mule, while in the case of the Naval Academy it was a goat. Moving the respective mascots across the country was a non-starter, so for Army we rented four mules from a national park, and for the Naval Academy they were able to fly in a six-month-old goat from Texas.

Both academies were pretty particular about the specifications of their mascots. The Navy's goat had to be a white angora - a breed that sounds fancy, but smells as bad as any other goat. The mule had to be 14 hands high with an "A" dyed on a shaved area on its rump. The academies got what they wanted, but there's a long and interesting story associated with the Navy goat.

I had learned that a Marine Battalion that then stationed in Lebanon had a pet goat. I wanted to get that goat from Lebanon, because it had already received some good press. That meant flying the goat from Lebanon to New York to Pasadena. Curiously, several airlines expressed a willingness to make that happen, probably by virtue of Naval Academy alumni in positions of both responsibility and influence (remember the importance of relationships and relationship-building). Pan Am had agreed to fly it from Lebanon to New York, and it looked like we were a-go.

The goat was loaded up and transported to JKF in New York City, and I thought everything was well in hand when I received another interrupter: a phone call to say that the Department of Agriculture was about to euthanize the goat because of concerns over hoof-and-mouth disease. Bringing a live goat into the United States was just not going to happen. I made an appeal directly to the Secretary of Agriculture, never mind how I got to him, and he issued an order to the authorities at JFK to release the goat for travel. Unfortunately, before the order reached the appropriate officials, the goat had been euthanized. Ultimately, that goat was one of only three casualties in this entire campaign, and I still feel bad about it. But there was no time for grief. We moved on to plan B: bringing a goat from Texas.

The other two casualties, incidentally, were minor. One of the Army's Golden Parachutists lost control of his chute during an exhibition drop and suffered a concussion, with no lasting damage. I also count my Executive Assistant as another casualty. I'll describe that a little later, but she did not suffer lasting damage, either.

There's a postscript to the goat affair. The Lebanese goat had been promised to a local little girl after the game, and there was considerable publicity around the touching story of this little girl getting the goat she always wanted. Perhaps because of the publicity, the Department of Agriculture found the little girl a substitute goat. When the U.S. Secretary of Agriculture telephoned the little girl's home to tell her family the good news, they had no idea who he was. The Secretary of Agriculture doesn't have a particularly high profile in Pasadena, notwithstanding its superlative growing season.

An Array of Activities

I need to add that the ground transportation plan in Los Angeles was no simple undertaking, due to the fact that over 400 buses were involved and over 300 cars, the latter through the courtesy of Buick dealers. We were moving a lot of people for multiple purposes. As an example, we planned a day the night before the game at Disneyland. Disneyland had agreed to shut the park down for the Corp of Cadets and the Brigade of Midshipmen, their friends, and their dates. I should add that shutting the park down one night for such an exclusive event was no small undertaking either.

The Thursday night of Thanksgiving, we endured what could have been the biggest interrupter of the entire campaign: it began to rain. Although the rain fell heavily at times, it did not dampen the spirits of the Cadets and Midshipmen, who were now visiting the Los Angeles area and Disneyland and having the time of their lives. It stopped raining at approximately 3:00 in the morning - I know that because I was out there with them. But when the rain stopped, it became apparent what an interrupter it had been. It threatened the march onto the field.

Tradition holds that prior to the game, the Corp of Cadets and the Brigade of Midshipmen conduct a march onto the field, which is an amazing and spectacular event on telecasts of the Army-Navy game. Early on the morning of the game, we discussed the condition of the field with the Commandants of the Military Academy and the Naval Academy. In the wet conditions, a march by over 9,000 Cadets and Midshipmen would be a disaster. It would ruin the field for the game.

The absence of the march would be a major disappointment. So, I decided to work with what we had. The Corps of Cadets and the Brigade of Midshipmen had to move from their assembly area in Downtown Pasadena to the Rose Bowl for the game a tad over a mile. We packaged this movement for the news media as the Army-Navy March, and I got myself on local television to promote it. Great masses of Pasadenans turned out to watch, and a major disappointment was turned into a media event and a great success.

After the game itself, traditionally the academies had a dance, or in Cadet and Midshipmen terminology, a "hop" – we were not going to disappoint. Our challenge was to provide the same event in Pasadena. Therefore, we planned a post-game dance at the Pasadena Convention Center for the Corp of Cadets and another dance at a

17

downtown airport hotel for the Midshipmen. The challenge was that we had to find dates for the Cadets and the Midshipmen. Needless to say we mounted a major campaign, which is not as easy as it sounds. We were surprised at the number of young ladies who were interested in attending this event. They significantly exceeded our requirements.

We had a number of major events and activities, which preceded the game itself – all intended to generate excitement within the community. We wanted to give acknowledgement to our sponsors and to those folks who had made financial contributions and to have the biggest possible public relations impact in the Los Angeles area. We had a *Salute to the Stars* event, where we honored Bob Hope and for the first time the combined glee clubs sang "More Than a Memory" in his honor, which brought him to tears. I know this because I was sitting directly across from him.

We scheduled a coaches' breakfast. We conducted a band review with the two bands, we had a Governor's reception and dinner, and I am pleased to note that these events were all completely sold out.

On Wednesday, the 23rd of November, the planes were in the air; Cadets and Midshipmen were looking forward to a very special weekend in Pasadena, California and an Army-Navy game to be played in the Rose Bowl. The community was excited and I was as nervous as cat on a hot tin roof since I only had a very small staff, although I had an army of volunteers (not unlike independent contractors, but without pay).

We were in the ballroom of a major hotel at a major luncheon to welcome the Superintendents, the Commandants, the Athletic Directors, key leadership team members from both the academies, members of Congress, and local leaders and dignitaries. Was it time for another interrupter? Indeed. My assistant handed me a note about one of the airlines that was programmed to bring Cadets from Stewart Field in Newburgh, and from New York to Los Angeles. The airline had gone bankrupt and a judge had intervened and said that they were not going to take off until they were paid in full. At that particular time, on that particular day, and at that particular hour, I did not have the $285,000 that the airline was looking for to allow that flight to depart from Stewart Field.

After a number of frantic calls and pleas, I was incredibly able to find $285,000, get a wire transfer, and allow those aircraft under this particular charter airline to depart from Stewart Field. This was at the end of the planned sequence of flights rather than at the beginning. At the end of the day, they arrived in Los Angeles later than expected, but in time to meet their host families and to participate in various events and activities that we had planned.

Competing with the Olympics
The planning and conducting of the Army-Navy game move was at the very least a "rush." The multiplicity of tasks and skillsets required was also the stuff of which make for major headaches. Fundraising qualified for a headache not unlike a hurricane - it was, however, an imperative. Raising $6 million dollars in less than 8 months while on imperative was no one's idea of a good time, never mind in direct competition with the Olympic

19

Organization Committee and the summer of '84 games in Los Angeles.

There had to be a niche, never mind very compelling campaign with an obvious target of the Defense Industry. It came down to hit lists and who knew the decider. I leveraged every relationship I had and more often than not, it was a two-man team making direct contact. Needless to say, at that level I had no choice but to be there. The bottom line was that 90% was in my head because, aside from the proposal, we did not have time for written detective plans. My brain was essentially captured in a three-ring binder, which quickly grew to 5 or 6 inches that I carried with me everywhere. By the way, this so spooked my newly formed Board that they took out an insurance policy on me for $10 million with Lloyds of London.

Clearly, before we launched on the visits for selecting sponsors, two things had to happen: first, a definition of benefits for the sponsors, and second, a major media effort to publicize the fact that the Army-Navy game was going to be played at the Rose Bowl. The downside then cut into the 8 months we had to raise the money. However, I then say a little bit like combat, when you soften the enemy up with proprietary fires before you attack. In that context, I could live with it. Obviously and cleverly, the Defense Industry was not our only target – we took aim at the graduates of the two academies who were CEO's of companies. They, however, were not as easy as it sounded because many thought, "it could not be done."

One of our biggest interrupters was playing the game the first Saturday in December. Fundraising for the Army-Navy game was launched almost exactly at the same time as the Olympic Organizing Committee was raising money for the Olympic summer games in Los Angeles in July of 1984. It goes without saying that the Olympic Organizing Committee had a little bit of a leg up on us because they were talking about sponsors for roughly a year of visibility. We were talking about one day of visibility.

Therefore, it should be no surprise that the cash went to the Olympic Organizing Committee, while the Army-Navy Game Foundation got pledges. Those pledges were to be paid in the first week of January 1984, which obviously put it into another fiscal year, meaning it would be manageable for our corporate sponsors. Since our payments – to airlines, hotels, vendors, suppliers, and others - would be 30 days from the date of the game, it meant our pledges would be paid in the same week that we needed the money for our bills.

That same evening of Wednesday, the 23rd of November, I had planned a Governor's reception and dinner, which highlighted the Governor of the State of California, members of the Senate, and the California House, and our local representatives. My plan was to make a presentation to the Governor, to our Senators, to our member of Congress, to the Academies a blown up version of the program for the Army-Navy game, which I must tell you I had a hand in designing. The cover was a Cadet carrying the Corp of Cadets flag and a Midshipman carrying the Brigade of Midshipmen flag while literally standing in the center of the Rose Bowl itself, all of which was superimposed on the flag of the State of California.

At about 3:00 in the morning on the day of the game, I encountered an interrupter that hit me quite personally: it was a call from the Chief of Police. His officers had found my Executive Assistant wandering the streets of Pasadena, not knowing who or where she was. She had suffered a complete breakdown. Such was the stress and the intensity of effort that had gone into making this event a reality. The impact of trying to overcome one obstacle after another can wear out even the strongest of us, and in this case, and to my extreme regret, it was my Executive Assistant. Happily, after a couple of days of rest, she recovered, and I know to this day feels that in some measure she had failed us. Needless to say, we extended special effort to call more attention to her many accomplishments and the obstacles that she had overcome, as opposed to one last obstacle or hurdle and that was getting the plaques to us for a presentation. In the great sum of things, it was a small thing indeed, especially since we made the presentations the following day during the course of the football game over in the Rose Bowl itself. Frankly, nobody knew the difference.

As far as the game itself goes, I am still trying to forget it. The Navy Receiver caught the opening kickoff at the 5-yard line, ran six yards, was about to be tackled and handed off to the Navy Tailback Napoleon McCallum who then sprinted the remaining 89 yards into the end zone for the first touchdown of the game. It was a prophetic play and more or less predicted what would actually happen: Navy went on to win. Not exactly what I had hoped for.

To add insult to the injury of Army fans, a group of Midshipmen had changed the HOLLYWOOD sign that is a prominent fixture in the Los Angeles area. They draped it with printed covers so that it read, "Beat Army."

Despite my disappointment with the game, I try to look at the event from 40,000 feet. The Army-Navy game had been successfully moved from Philadelphia to the Rose Bowl and the entire Corp of Cadets and the Brigade of Midshipmen, football teams, coaches, fans, official parties, and all were transported back to the respective academies completely on time and successfully. This event has become part of their memory book and I continue to run into Cadets and Midshipmen who were there on the 25th of November 1983, when the game was played in the Rose Bowl.

Over 80,000 people attended the Army-Navy Rose Bowl game that Friday afternoon. That figure significantly eclipsed previous attendance at the game, never mind the fact that it was being conducted on the day after Thanksgiving in California, not Philadelphia.

Unable to Overcome the Final Obstacle

Unfortunately, the story does not end there. I noted at the beginning of this prologue that sometimes you engage an obstacle that your best efforts might not overcome because somebody else is deciding the outcome. Our biggest obstacle arose after the game to spoil our triumph.

The following Monday November 27, 1983, Senator Proxmire asked that an investigation be conducted into the Army-Navy game to determine whether any federal money had been used to transport the Corp of Cadets and the Brigade of Midshipmen. The *Los Angeles Times* came out with a headline piece that essentially read that the Army-Navy game under investigation. I don't have to tell you the impact that had on all those pledges that we were anticipating that first week of January. All that any prospective donor, particularly in the corporate community, would have to see is that the game was tainted in some way. Many opted to withhold payment on their pledges. This was not a pretty picture. The air went out of the balloon. It removed much of the sense of accomplishment and excitement our team had from successfully mounting this undertaking. It hardly mattered that we were later exonerated either.

We really didn't have that much money to make payment to the airlines, never mind the hotels, for bus transportation, and for the various other costs that made up a $6 million budget. There is some satisfaction that our initial budget estimates were right on target. The expense side of the balance sheet was within one percent of our estimates. Obviously, the revenue side had fallen short and very specifically where donations were to come into play.

After nine months, the investigation concluded that the money spent was primarily focused on transporting the Corp of Cadets from West Point to Stewart Field in Newburgh, New York and the Brigade of Midshipmen from Annapolis to nearby Baltimore and to the airport. On an annual basis this is a typical expenditure. While no government money had been expended, at the end of the day the damage to our reputation had an unbelievable impact on our ability to call in the pledges, and we were short a significant amount of monies. Monies owed not only to the hotels, but to the bus companies, airlines and various other vendors and providers.

We set about a mammoth undertaking to settle those claims as best as we could and to utilize those results of the GAO investigation, Government Accounting Office, as a vehicle to re-plea our case for pledge monies. Sometimes successfully so, but more often than not it wasn't too successful. This was now a long gone event nine months later, and from a sponsor perspective there was not much to be gained in honoring a pledge. Yes, they had received the recognition as a sponsor, but that recognition was our only leverage in settling the claims. However, this did not stop the Secretary of the Navy in his lawsuit against the Foundation and against myself as well as my co-chair, Robert Finch.

We found it sort of amazing that we would be personally named in the suit since we had the coverage of the Foundation behind us. But nevertheless, it led to many restless days and many sleepless nights, as well as considerable anguish. Obviously, there was a whole new obstacle: where do we find the monies for the legal fees to fight this issue? My co-chairman was a senior partner in a law firm and by definition could not participate in this undertaking. At best, I was flying on one year of law that I took in my senior year at West Point. The depositions were finally concluded that I had to participate in had a depth of in excess of 10 inches. While in my heart of hearts, I wanted to see all those monies paid, but this was one obstacle that we could not overcome.

After multiple attempts through the United States District Court in California, the lawsuit was dismissed in June of 1985, almost two years after the game itself. While my co-chair and I were relieved, given the bigger picture, interest in admissions west of the Mississippi (specifically in the California area) skyrocketed for the two academies. I can tell you this because I chaired a selection committee for a local member of Congress and was in touch with other members of the congress in

California and their admissions committees and the number of applicants absolutely soared.

The goodwill in the City of Pasadena among the host families will endure for years to come. The City of Philadelphia now has to allow the game to move out of Philadelphia once every five years and, while not to the west coast or to the southwest or to the southeast, it has been able to move all the same. The game has been played in Baltimore and Washington D.C. and Giants Stadium in New York City with considerable success and great attendance.

The biggest lesson I learned from overcoming the many, many obstacles that came along with moving the Army-Navy game is to always have a plan B, or to be quick on your feet and ready with an alternative course of action. Sometimes failure is not an option. Yet, to this day, we were not able to pay 100 percent of the monies owed. That is one obstacle that we could not clear. When I was at West Point as a Cadet, they used to say, "There may be a reason, but there's never an excuse."

In the Second Punic War, 200 years before the Christian era, Hannibal achieved three signal victories against the Roman armies, at Trebia, Trasimene, and Cannae. Trasimene was the greatest ambush in history, and the Romans lost six soldiers for every Punic soldier killed. Cannae is known as the scene of history's first pincer movement, and resulted in the loss of ten Romans for each one Hannibal lost. Hannibal is without doubt one of the greatest Generals who ever lived. But if you ask anyone what he's famous for, the chances are very good they will tell you he crossed the Alps with elephants.

Hannibal's victories were spectacular and his generalship brilliant, but his crowning achievement was in moving his army from one place to another. This is one of those places in which history is correct. Troop movements and logistics don't attract as much interest as battles, but they are often more decisive and sometimes harder to execute. History doesn't have much to say about Hannibal's planning for the Second Punic War, but I think it must have been one of the greatest planning exercises in history.

Moving the Army-Navy game to the Rose Bowl was a small thing compared to the Second Punic War, but I hope you have been amazed at the effort that went into planning it. I have to admit that the very idea of making it happen was exhilarating and it kept me moving on a day-to-day basis. Each day I tried to "get to yes" and avoid being concerned by those who were skeptical, told me it couldn't be done or they just thought it was a lousy idea. I fondly remember visits to both West Point and Annapolis to meet with their leadership teams, not to mention visiting the Pentagon. One of the high points of my career at that point was having lunch with the Secretary of the Air Force in his dining room, where we thought "out of the box" and came up with ways to overcome the objections of the Secretary of the Navy, who was a native of Philadelphia.

Although moving the game was not the financial success I had hoped it would be, it was still one of the peak experiences of my professional life. Hannibal's achievement of crossing the Alps with an army is still impressive today, and I yield to no one in my admiration of it. However, I would like to point out that my campaign of moving the Army-Navy game had fewer casualties.

Chapter 1

Why Is Finishing so Hard?

In the modern business world, we're very good at starting. What we're not so good at is finishing. That's why I say, "Start everything, finish nothing" should be the motto of the modern workplace. How did we get into this state of affairs?

On any given day, we confront a list of tasks that need to be completed, and as we work away at these (sometimes even before we finish reviewing the list), more are added. The reality is that new tasks are going to be added faster than you can finish the existing ones – that's just the way it is. The trick is to finish the important tasks. Finishing these tasks requires intense discipline, because the important tasks are invariably the hard ones.

Most of us have so little control over that list of tasks that we are forced to work first, not on the ones that are important, but on the ones that have the closest deadline. Attach a clock to it, and the task automatically goes to the top of the list. This has to be done by 5:00 p.m. That has a deadline of tomorrow. The workday comes to resemble a sporting event, two-minute warning and all. But that's where the resemblance ends, because we never get far

28

enough ahead to follow a strategy of running out the clock – we are always desperate to beat it.

Even there, many of us call "overtime," but you can't call overtime unless there's a tie to be broken - how often does that actually happen? In business, as in life, there are not too many tiebreakers or opportunities to improve on the quality of the product or the level of the service. We should all be fans of doing it right the first time and on time. I don't often see that in taglines or in contracts, but maybe that's why there are over 1.5 million bankruptcies in the U.S. each year.

In business, we all have annual business and budget plans. We have a series of goals that are well defined and the finish line is normally December 31st, but it's not a real finish line. It's a ribbon stretched across the track by your CPA and the IRS – meaningful only to them. It has very little to do with you. In fact, there is a tomorrow and that's January 1st or next week or next month. My At-A-Glance annual calendar has January of next year right after December of this year. I love it because it reminds me that I'm not finished. While my CPA and the IRS are wrapping up a package full of what I've done in the last 12 months, I have to keep going.

Each chapter of this book identifies a reason why finishing is so hard, and we will get to those reasons as they arise. But before we do, I want to give you the view from 40,000 feet.

Now Firing
No matter what forces are trying to prevent you from finishing, you need to be able first to define "finish." Here's something I hate: I'm in a restaurant, and a waiter

comes up and says, "Are you still working on that?" Maybe there's still food on my plate, but what an awful question to ask. Why do they want to make the meal seem like work? I would prefer they asked, "Are you still enjoying your meal?"

Think of your workday as a restaurant meal. At the end of the day, ask yourself, "Am I still having fun?" If not, maybe it's time to let them take the plate away.

All of us have seen the "NOW HIRING" signs that are so prevalent when the local economy is growing. That sign is encouraging for someone looking for a job. It means the company is growing and new people are needed to meet the increased demand and take the company to the next level, or it could mean someone has quit, retired, or been fired. I read some research in the 1970's that said the majority of firings took place because of organizational cultural issues, and I wonder if that is still true 40 years later. I have become more and more concerned that too many think that work ethic is a name of a California rock group.

How often have you been on the interstate or the freeway and some genius cuts you off? Instead of screaming at him or here, maybe I should hire him – here is someone who wants to get to work!

We've all seen people in the workplace who are simply lazy. Work per se is not their thing. They will do or meet the minimum expectation and are just not motivated. This is why I like preseason football. Everyone has to compete for their position until they get down to 53. This is really no different in baseball, except they can be sent to the farm club and work their way back. Baseball, however, is the only profession I know where the goal is to get it right 30% of the time. I think the workplace should be like preseason football. I think you should put a sign on the building that says, "NOW FIRING." This tells your employees that they have to battle for their position every day. Several times in my career I have avoided firing bad employees, and it came back and bit me every time. I lost credibility in those situations. I've even lost good employees because I failed to fire a bad one.

Frankly, I hate firing but, more often than not, it turns out to be the best thing that could happen for them and for the business. Needless to say, I don't want the organization to develop a culture of fear. If you fire people as often as you need to, and you don't want to create a culture of fear, you need to enlist three powerful forces:

- Accountability.
- Motivation.
- Strong lines of communication.

Make Them, and Yourself, Accountable

If things are going to get finished, nevertheless in a timely manner, you have to hold your employees, as well as yourself, accountable. Assign tasks one at a time for them to complete. In the Army, there was a simple term: "what gets done is what the commander inspects." Daily huddles, walking the four corners, dashboard reports, and key indicators should be part of your routine. You have to keep your eye on the "ball" – your people. Try not looking at the ball in any sport and you see what does not happen.

How often do projects or tasks fall behind? We all know the reason, but what did we do about it? I can assure you there are always consequences. Those consequences can include reduced profit, or even no profit, or even a lost contract or customer. What is missing of course is do you hold yourself accountable? "I will get to it later or tomorrow" and "That's going to have to be good enough" are not the kinds of remarks that bespeak accountability. No matter how high you rise in an organization, you still need to find ways to challenge yourself. I worked with Vistage, the world's leading chief executive organization, and when we asked our CEO membership what they wanted from the Vistage experience, virtually all of them replied with "to be held accountable." The world hungers for accountability – if you provide it, you will prosper.

At some level I am challenging you, the reader, to make the most of every day and don't let your head hit the pillow unless you can say, "I got something of measurable value done today." Nothing surprises me more than decision makers that cannot make a decision. CEO, president, manager, whatever... if it's in your job description to make decisions, then make decisions. President Harry Truman had a sign on his desk that read, "The buck stops here." Now there's a man who declared himself the decider and meant it.

It does not make any difference where you are on the ladder of success. Someone is looking to you to make a decision. You've heard the phrase "it is lonely at the top." This is just another way of saying it is up to you. Clearly, some decisions are more difficult than others, and a day does not go by when decisions large and small have to be and are being made.

The bottom line is that you have to decide to decide on stuff or it just simply will not get done. In the prologue of this book, I explained how I decided that the Army-Navy game should be played in the Rose Bowl in Pasadena, California. My wife told me it could not be done; yet as you found out in my account, obviously it was.

The Lower Right-Hand Double-Drawer

As a Lieutenant, I was privileged to be the aide-de-camp to the Commanding General of Fort Riley Kansas in the 10th Infantry Division. For all practical purposes, I was his Executive Assistant. He had an interesting habit – he liked to clear his desk completely before somebody came in to see him, so all matter of papers and studies would be swept from the top of his desk and wind up in that lower right-hand double-drawer. The bad news is they never came out. One day he called me in and said, "I'd like you to empty that drawer, put it in a box, take it out and burn it." Needless to say, I was aghast, but I did as ordered, and it turned out to be kind of funny. There was absolutely no repercussion, no outcry – no "where is that study?" no "what are we going to be doing next?"

However, there was one piece of paper that fell under the title of a controlled document – it was an Officer's efficiency report that the General had to sign. Not unlike a job performance report, these are closely tracked, and when it didn't appear, the path led to that double drawer. There is a point in all this and that is sometimes we get overwhelmed with busy work, which has little or no purpose. Here is a little test you can perform to decide whether you should start a project. Ask these two questions:

- Is it likely this project will never be completed?
- Is this project irrelevant to your goals?

If you answer either question with a "yes," this project is a candidate for death in the lower right-hand double-drawer.

Sometimes you may work on a project for an extended period of time, only to conclude it can't be done; it might be a lack of cash or resources, or more likely, it simply comes down to your people. This is where your leadership team comes into play. Assuming that you have selected the right people and motivated them, they will respond to your direction or they will form a group in a think-tank type environment and identify ways to overcome the obstacles. If properly motivated, they see it as a challenge and an opportunity and not a reason to give up.

A Template for Difficult Problems
The Vistage process uses a template to deal with a difficult decision. The template is a sort of checklist that reduces the problem into manageable components. First you name the issue concisely. You must be able to get to the heart of the problem in one to two sentences. Is it a concern? Is it a challenge? Is it an opportunity, a problem, or a personal issue?

Next, you concisely describe its significance. What are the effects on dollars, people, products, services, customers, family, time, and the future?

Also, what is the ideal outcome? Is this what you really want to see happen?

Now, provide relevant background: bullet points on how, when, why, where it started, who the players are, what forces are at work, today's status, future impact, and so on.

Next, what have you done up to this point? What are the various options you have considered? What actions have you taken or plan to take?

Finally, what help do you want from the rest of the team – possible solutions? Possible alternatives? The identification of consequences? Where to find more information? Critique the current plan?

Using this format can be very helpful in soliciting input so that you make better and faster decisions. You can even use the checklist to ask yourself the questions without taking the problem to your leadership team.

I should point out that in any discussion by your leadership team when you're addressing decisions of this matter, the expected procedure is to go around the table to each person allowing them to ask a question and then you go on to the next. This process will only scratch the surface, and since you have already scratched the surface, it isn't going to help you. You need to drill deeper.

Drill deeper with each team member: after a member asks his or her question, and before you move to the next individual, you look at what that person has asked and ask if anybody can take it down another level. Every problem is an onion, and you have to peel each layer away to find the layer beneath.

This process quite often breaks the problem down into more manageable tasks and goals, then you can do it in steps or phases using the resources you have. Track what you're doing on a whiteboard - I'm a huge fan of whiteboards. By writing each thing you know about the problem on the whiteboard, you actually can see what's missing. You've probably seen them use whiteboards this way on the detective shows on TV. The detectives stand in front of a whiteboard, writing down facts and drawing relationships, and bit-by-bit the pieces start coming together. It sits there for anyone to glance at as they walk by until someone eventually sees what is missing.

In the initial stages of problem solving, your operating principle is there is no such thing as a bad idea; some are just better than others. If you start qualifying ideas in the early stages, you start cutting off paths to the solution. Soon, you have nowhere to go.

What Happens When You Give Up

Over multiple careers, I've seen the good, the bad, and the ugly. I've been the staff guy looking up the ladder and the one being looked up to when I was in the position of leadership. From both the top and the bottom, the lesson I always learned was, "don't give up." I have been in positions where the decision was not mine, and the obstacles were deemed too great to overcome. That can be tough when you believe there has to be a way to make it work, but then I assumed that those guys up the line knew more than I did. I just never knew what it was that they knew that I didn't.

I learned my approach to obstacles in high school. At the age of 9, I decided that I wanted to go to West Point. By my senior year in high school, I was selected as the first alternate for entrance to the Academy, but unfortunately, my principal got accepted. That only drove me to another level of intensity that pushed me to seek every path that I could, which would ultimately lead me to admission a year later into West Point. I received a very practical lesson in obstacles when I was there. Every Cadet had to complete the IOCT, or Indoor Obstacle Course Test, every year. It is a sequence of 11 tests: low crawl under barrier, tire footwork, two-handed vault, 8-foot horizontal shelf, horizontal bar navigation, hanging tire, balance beam, 8-foot horizontal wall, 20-foot horizontal ladder, 16-foot vertical rope, and 350-meter sprint (carrying a 6-pound medicine ball for the first 120 meters, a baton for the second 120 meters, and empty-handed for the remaining 110 meters). Even fit Cadets will spend hours coughing and wheezing after completing it, a condition called "Hayes lung," for the gymnasium in which the course is housed. For me, there was a 12th obstacle, which was keeping my lunch down. Every time I crossed the finish line of that course, I promptly threw up.

In my career, both in the Army and in the business world, I faced the situation many times when I was a subordinate and someone above me made the decision not to proceed on a project. It gives you an unpleasant, empty feeling. I wondered then how I would feel when the decision was mine, and finally when it was up to me, it was not as easy as I thought. It's funny how that works. As hard as it is, however, I would suggest you don't give up on a project. Just find a way to get it done. You don't want your subordinates to get that unpleasant, empty feeling, because that's a reflection on you.

When you're looking for another way to get it done, don't fall into the trap of taking the project back from someone you assigned it to. It's all too easy to conclude that if it is going to get done it is easier if you do it yourself. I'm sure you've heard (or even said) this: "By the time I explain it to someone else, I can do it faster and better." Really? I have been there more often than I can tell you.

Being in business today is a lot like being in combat, but without all the noise. Someone out there wants to kill you (take your business away) or at least shoot at you (undermine your credibility, you can't deliver on time or get it right the first time). In combat, as in business, when you have good people, you give them both responsibility and the authority. You let them make decisions, and you have their back – and they have yours.

The Importance of Training

Delegation failures tend to happen because we haven't done the necessary advance work. What is the advance work? Preparing people to take on the tasks we delegate to them. Almost all businesses are woefully weak in training their people to improve their existing skill sets or get them to the next level. The reasons are legion: no money, can't tolerate lost time, or worst of all, someone will steal your best talent. Whatever happens in your business, you can be sure of one thing: it's going to change. If it changes, then by definition your people have to change - that change is known as learning. When you provide your people with training, you provide them with learning opportunities. Ask yourself this question: do you want your doctor, your dentist, or your lawyer to stop learning? Of course not.

Change can take you off of your game plan – it is more often than not disruptive and can make it difficult to focus. It can be as simple as an interruption, which forces you to change what you were doing, or it can be a change of mind by a superior or a customer with the dreaded change order. It can be a resignation by a key employee where replacement is a difficult and timely undertaking. It can be an assumption that proved false, or it can be your banker calling to tell you that your line of credit has been lowered. It can be a new way of doing business that you must master to stay competitive.

The answer is to avoid "Ready, fire, aim." Step back, think it through, consult with others, and then commit to action. Change cannot be ignored. You have to deal with it and say to yourself, "bring it on!" Your ability to manage and control your time is an imperative. In working with CEOs and senior executives, I asked them, how do you allocate your time? Do you increase your hours from 50 to 60 or do you readdress how and where you are spending your time? Candidly, the biggest waste of my time is appointment changes. I am obviously a dying breed. If you were on the calendar, you were on the calendar. That's it. Needless to say, everyone strives for work/life balance and most fail. There is no silver bullet, but you must start with establishing priorities, having protected time, and having a defined goal or as appropriate a sub-goal.

It goes without saying that you have to allocate time for meetings, as well as communicating with your employees and your direct reports. That's just part of the job. Of course, the key is that you have to have protected time so you could work your own to-do list: this is an area you must not give up.

Someone appears in the doorway of your office and asks, "Are you busy?" Of course I am! But I came in knowing that a part of my day was going to be given to others. They were looking for approval in their quest to finish what they started, or they were looking for the answer to the question, "What should I do?" I never gave them the answer to that. I would reverse the question back to them to force them to come up with the solution. They were closer to the problem than I was, and nine times out of 10 they knew what was needed. They just wanted reaffirmation. This is always the best option, but if the solution falls short this leaves me with two options: I could modify the decision but leave them with ownership of the problem or, less desirably, I could challenge their thinking to guide them in a new direction. The downside is the cost ownership, and at some level, passion. Candidly, don't you have the same problem at home?

When it comes to time and commitment, I'm a bit of a nut case. When I was in the Army and we would be reassigned, whether it was from the Far East or from Europe back to the United States, we would generally have our orders about six months out. More often than not it meant cross country travel and at least five to seven days on the road to our destination and new assignment. We use this as an opportunity to visit friends along the way. It was certainly more fun than staying in a hotel or a motel by virtue of the many classmates that I grew to know and serve with in multiple locations, in addition to the people that I've met along the way.

We had friends virtually in every city across the country. Six months in advance, I would tell them that we plan to arrive at their home on a given date at a given time (usually in the late afternoon) and that we would be leaving at a given time on a given date. Recall what I just said: I would do these things six months out. Well, guess what? On that day and at that time we would pull up in their driveway. They could never figure out how we did that. To them it was a miracle, some act of God. How could I possibly tell them six months out that I would be in their driveway at a given time on a given date? Frankly, it's not very complicated – I knew where I was coming from, and I knew where I was going. I knew how long it was going to take between those two places and I made a commitment and we kept it. Not unlike the person you send a reminder to about a time and place to meet, where they have scheduled something else and did not tell you until the follow-up, and then got the "oops" message — speaks to commitment, doesn't it?

If there is an imperative in working, selling yourself or a product, networking, building relationships in business or at home, it is to listen. Never lose an opportunity to listen. Every effective leader knows that listening accomplishes two things: 1) it brings in useful information and 2) it raises the receptivity of the person you're listening to. That's why you always listen to your subordinates, your customers, your spouse, and your children. You cannot view them as interrupters — you must view as them as sources of the information that is going to improve the quality of your decisions and as vital connections you need to survive and flourish. The failure to listen can keep you from your goal because you went down the wrong path or you started something without all the facts, or lost the loyalty of someone you needed.

Protect Your Time
Even while you honor the imperative to listen, you have to find ways to protect your own time. Here's one little trick I use: I have always had an open door policy. What I found is that if I remained seated behind my desk when someone came in, they would in turn seat themselves in front of me. A seated person is more difficult to dislodge than a standing one by an order of magnitude. My habit when anyone comes in is to stand up. They read that as a form of respect, which of course they love, but I don't stop there. I come around to the other side of the desk and meet with them on their side. There were two benefits to

this. One, there is no desk between the two of you, which means there is one less obstacle to good communication. Two, you can decide when the conversation is over. Just start walking to the door and they will go with you. If you value your time, this one trick could justify the purchase price of this book the first time you use it.

You can't use that trick on the phone, of course, so here's another one. Use this only in when you're desperate to get off the phone with someone who won't let you go: as soon as you can take your turn talking (or even if you have to interrupt the other person), start talking and then hang up on yourself mid-sentence – they will think they got disconnected.

Ok. Back to getting stuff done. It's 4:00 p.m. What did you start? What did you finish? Hopefully you checked off a few priority tasks. No way does it all get done; stuff just happens. If it is a Monday, you can move it to Tuesday, or since you are a 24/7 person you can deal with it later. I love someone who sends me a message at 2:00 a.m. to tell me they'll be late for our 7:30 morning breakfast. I gave up keeping my laptop under my pillow. It gave me a headache.

I tend to launch early and check my messages when I get to my first meeting destination. My assumption is that I'm going to be there, so they certainly will be there as well. Well, that does not always happen. A couple of lessons learned here, the first of which being to take five minutes before you leave to check your messages. There's no telling if someone is having one of those "what keeps you awake at night" moments. One of those could be they suddenly realized that hidden in their handheld device is a breakfast meeting with you. Those same 24/7 night owls may finally be responding to your message that you sent during daylight hours or before you went to bed. Here's another hint: don't ask two questions in the same message because chances are they will only answer the one on top. In the middle of the night (and many other times as well), people are either too tired to scroll down or in a hurry to respond. Of course, that doesn't even mean they will answer fully the question they are responding to.

I have also learned to take work with me when I'm away from the office. If I'm early or they are late or, God forbid, they didn't check their calendars or that handheld device generally located at the end of their arm, my time is not wasted and I just won time to deal with uncompleted or in-progress tasks. By the way, in addition to having my iPhone, I carry a printed calendar with me. As a result, *I don't miss meetings*. I know what you're thinking as you read this, but it works. Pure and simple, I am a planner. I operate by the principle that if I don't know where I'm going, I won't know when I get there!

Why is finishing so hard? It's because of *you*. At the end of the day, you have four imperatives:

- Prioritize.
- Stay the course.
- Focus.
- Protect your time.

If you don't honor the four imperatives, you will not meet your goals, whatever they may be. I know. I was urged to write this book over five years ago. What stopped me? Because I knew I would start everything and finish nothing.

Chapter 2

"It Can't Be Done"

Oh yes, it can be done, but only if you decide it can. At the beginning of this book I noted that we start everything and finish nothing - much of the time this is because we don't make the decision to finish. When I talk about making a decision here, I don't mean it in the way most people mean it. Most people talk about making a decision with the real meaning being picking an alternative from two or more courses of action. Picking the alternative, however, is only the first part of making a decision – you haven't finished making the decision until you have committed yourself to that alternative. This is the part that requires serious effort.

Everyone wants to lose weight, to exercise more, and to improve their work-life balance, so why are so few people successful in reaching these goals? I think it's because few people actually make the decision to achieve the goal. They may choose a more slender figure, a higher level of fitness, or a more balanced life, but that's as far as it goes. They make the choice, but not the commitment. The commitment requires self-discipline and accountability to the self.

The first year I tried for West Point, I was in a prep school. I was a junior, and like everybody else, I was looking to determine what college or university I was going to go to. However, it was an easy choice for me. As I briefly mentioned before, when I was nine years old, I visited West Point, decided it was the place I wanted to be, and never questioned myself from then onward.

The good news is that I was fortunate enough to get a first alternate position. In those days, a member of Congress could appoint a principal and three alternates. That meant that if the principal did not go, I was next in line.

The principal did in fact make it, and so I was dead in the water. However when he got to West Point, he resigned in less than 60 days – it goes without saying that I was beyond angry and frustrated. This anger and frustration caused me to move from choice to decision. At least in my mind, I had lost a year, but I set about exploring every option. I worked harder, I became more physically fit, I improved my grades, and I continued to pursue a Congressional appointment.

Having stepped over the line from choice to decision, having – in other words – committed myself to this goal, before the year was out I was in the competition for a Congressional appointment to West Point, a Congressional appointment to the Naval Academy, and Senatorial appointments to each as well. I had also applied to University of California at Berkeley and to UCLA.

I had focused myself so completely on a principal appointment to West Point that I swept up a lot of other goals as well. When I got my principal appointment to

West Point, I also had the opportunity for a principal appointment to the Naval Academy, acceptance for admission to UCLA, and acceptance for admission to University of California at Berkeley. That taught me the difference between a choice and a decision. That taught me the power of commitment as well as the value of multiple courses of action. I flat out didn't give up and chose to see this additional year as an opportunity to achieve my goals.

What Has to Be Done, Can Be Done

I was off to West Point, and I wasn't the only one who made the commitment. A year after I entered West Point, my original principal appointee reapplied. I could hardly wait to pounce on him when he arrived at West Point, and I spent a year making his life as miserable as I could. We eventually became very good friends, but that's another story.

Here is part of what prepared me to make my commitment: during my high school years, I was fortunate in the summer time to have a lifeguard position at the La Jolla Beach and Tennis Club. As lifeguards, every morning we had to prove ourselves. We had swim out to a raft, cross over to another one, and swim back in to shore. The raft was a long way off. As I stood on the beach every morning I told myself, just as did the others, that it couldn't be done. But clearly, it had to be done. Failing to complete the swim offered multiple opportunities for drowning or, what's worse for a high school kid, getting rescued. I'm happy to tell you that my confidence grew enormously over those summers as every morning I made that swim, and it was no longer an obstacle or a challenge, but the opportunity to tell myself on a daily basis, "Yes, I can do this."

In your first year at West Point, they separate those who can from those who can't very, very quickly. I entered the Military Academy on the 1st of July 1949. On the 4th of July, we were told that we were going to go on a scenic tour of West Point's historical buildings and the Academy's many places of interest, which would allow us to familiarize ourselves with our new home.

The morning of the tour, we were told to put on full combat gear and assemble in the area outside of our barracks. Once in formation, we were ordered to fix bayonets. Then it was, "Forward, march!" Followed by, "Double-time!"

The double time march is approximately twice the speed of the regular march. It is about 180 paces per minute – not quite a sprint, but faster than a jog. As we double-timed around West Point, when we encountered a point of interest, we were given the command "Eyes right!" Without stopping, we were advised on what building we were looking at. Then we would be quickly given the command "Ready front!" and continued to the next point of interest.

It wasn't very long into this scenic tour of West Point that I began to hear a tiny voice in my head saying, "It can't be done." I am sure everyone else heard the same voice, but stopping the march (AKA the "scenic tour") was not an option offered to us. It took two and a half hours at a running march with full gear and fixed bayonets to see all the points of interest. To this day, I wouldn't be able to tell you what any of those points of interest were – all I remember is the exhaustion afterward.

Breaking a Big Thing into Smaller Things

Plebe, or freshman, gymnastics was somewhat the same way. In our first year, we had to experience 24 hours of gym, 24 hours of boxing, 24 hours of wrestling, and 24 hours of swimming. When we got to the gymnasium, we were told to sit on the floor. When our instructors came out in their AAA tee shirts (Army Athletic Association), they looked like a bunch of gorillas.

These instructors began going through routines on the equipment, and they looked like what you see when you watch the Summer Olympics and gymnastics. I had never in my wildest dreams seen myself on the horse or the parallel bars or tumbling or on the high bar. We watched our instructors fly through this equipment, and you can guess what the tiny voice was saying? "It can't be done."

However, here lies the interesting part. We took each series of exercises with each piece of equipment in a carefully crafted sequence of events, so that each one built on the other. We grew in confidence and ability, so that when all the 24 hours were complete, we had navigated every one of those pieces of equipment and accomplished the impossible. In later years, I have watched the Summer Olympics, and I remember my plebe year and now the tiny voice says, "What was so hard about that?"

Boxing was a whole other issue. I hated boxing. As a kid in first grade, I was on a teeter-totter, and I was up while the other kid was down when the bell rang. He took off instantly, and I went down with the upper end of the teeter-totter. Unfortunately, the bar caught me right in the face, resulting in a very bloody nose. To this day one side of my nose is a little bit sensitive (maybe I should say a lot sensitive). This experience made me very wary of blows to the nose.

I would get in the ring at West Point for plebe boxing, and it wouldn't be very long before my opponent would tag me on the right side of my face. If he caught my nose, I was an instant bloody mess. Everybody would assume the match was over at that point.

Personally, I was kind of used to this and, bloody nose notwithstanding, I would continue to box. It can be disquieting to box with someone who is bleeding all over you, and I think the blood so intimidated my opponents that in the end I won more matches than I lost. Winning never made me like it though.

The Value of Preparation

My experience as a lifeguard and the swim out to those rafts every day came into play when it was time for survival training. We were paired off, then it was decided that one partner was going to be the survivor and the other was going to conduct the rescue; I was very fortunate in the flip of the coin and I was going to play the role of the rescuer. The victim was of course told to battle just as strongly and as vigorously as they could to prevent being rescued.

By virtue of training, I was fortunately able to fight my classmate off, drag him in, and accomplished what I had set out to do. When our roles were reversed, he was unfortunately so tired and exhausted that he didn't make it and had to repeat that sequence, so that he would complete the requirements in swimming. The usefulness of my lifeguard background and proving myself every day of the summer taught me that you never know when preparation is going to pay off, so you should prepare yourself as well as you can for any situation.

Several years afterwards, I had graduated West Point and was given an assignment at Fort Riley, Kansas, where I was the Aide-de-Camp to the Commanding General. The Commanding General was being reassigned, and it was then appropriate for me to go back to troop duty as the new Commanding General would select his own aide. Back at my new regiment, the discussion went through the chain of command: "What are we going to do with this smart ass aide to show him that he's not going to be riding around in sedans with the Commanding General and having a lot of special privileges?"

They settled on sending me to the 5th Army Physical Training School, where they trained officers in teaching physical education and training. This physical training course was no cakewalk. The intent was that if you were going to lead soldiers in physical training, you had better be pretty fit yourself. Being totally prepared to run as far as you can run, do every one of the push-ups and the pull-ups, as well as the various exercises that you were going to teach them was a must.

I knew I had to outperform, and yet still I heard that tiny voice: "It can't be done." I found that one of the ways I could quiet that voice was to treat each day as a goal in itself. I convinced myself that I only had to get through a single day, and the assignment got done one day at a time. I'm a little embarrassed to admit that I finished each day totally exhausted and, on more than one occasion, threw up.

When it was over and time for graduation, I found that all those successful (and even vomit filled) days added up to something: I was the honor graduate. That graduation in itself was fun - because I was the honor graduate, the Regimental Commander had to attend the graduation ceremonies and present me with my graduation certificate. Nothing gave me greater pleasure than to see the look on his face as I stood there accepting that recognition. Without saying a word, I was able to look him squarely in the eye with an expression that said, "Don't ever tell me that there is something I can't do."

Implementing a New Army Training System

Much later in my military career, I had an assignment in research and development – I was charged with finding a way to utilize eye-safe lasers, which would be placed on the Army's family of direct fire weapons to get an indication of hit.

At that time I could not spell the word laser, but eventually I became the leading expert in the application of eye-safe lasers on the Army's family of direct fire weapons. The concept was to have detectors on soldiers and detectors on equipment, including tanks. The soldier would then fire his weapon using blank ammunition.

A device, not unlike a hearing aid, reacted to the noise of the weapon firing by triggering the laser. The laser would hit what the soldier was firing at. Each soldier wore a detector on his shoulder equipment (helmet or harness), and if the laser beam hit the detector, a buzzer went off to notify the soldier he'd been "killed." This truly brought to training a level of realism that it never had before.

If the laser missed nothing would happen, but a soldier with his buzzer going off had only one course of action: to silence the buzzer. He could only do this by pulling a pin, which disengaged his laser so that he was out of action.

Clearly, you can't kill a tank with a rifle. Therefore, if a soldier was firing his weapon at a tank, the system made an intermittent noise to alert someone in the tank that they were under fire but a kill was not possible. The only way that a kill could take effect was with an anti-tank gun, and a direct hit from that ignited a red smoke grenade.

I don't have to tell you the number of skeptics along the way who doubted that such a system could ever be put in place, never mind work. Along the way, some well-meaning meddler decided that we had to prove that the laser was eye-safe. What if a participant pointed a rifle towards the soldier's head, could it hit him in the eye?

While I don't suggest that you try this, it frankly can't be done. Nevertheless, we had to prove that if it could happen, there would be no damage to the retina. We were sidetracked while this was tested on rats, which triggered another outburst and another cry on the part of the rat protectors of the world.

Let me pause here for an interesting story. When we were working with the prototype of this system, it was called LES (laser engagement system). Unfortunately, that term was proprietary and we had to come up with another name.

I was with an old classmate of mine in the officer's club one night and we talked about what we were going to call this new system - both of us agreed that I had a boss who was more than deserving of having the system named in his honor. His first name was Myles, but no matter how hard we tried, we could not come up with a proper use for the letter Y. We finally landed on substituting the letter I, and came up with "MILES," meaning "Multiple Integrated Laser Engagement System." I can't imagine a more jumbled bunch of words with less meaning attached to them than that descriptor, all for what was about to become the Army's leading training system, which still endures today. However, what I have to tell you is that later we discovered "miles" is also a Greek word meaning foot soldier.

"I Work for Peanuts"

My job in Orlando was as president of a small consulting company. I had been successful in a proposal with the Florida Department of Agriculture for coming up with a campaign to promote the peanut industry in the state of Florida. Georgia, of course, owns the peanut industry for all intents and purposes. I had quite the challenge trying to figure out how you compete with somebody like Georgia and position Florida as being a force in peanut production. Once again, the tiny voice sounded: "It can't be done." In fact, there wasn't anybody around me that even came close to assuming that this could be done.

This all changed when I came up with idea to have a contest for a "Peanut Queen." As luck would have it, she was very small in stature, and when somebody commented on her selection I observed, "I think it's a distinct advantage for her to be promoting the peanut industry because if you take a look, she's really peanut sized."

We also put together a peanut butter and jelly sandwich lunch for the state legislature in Tallahassee, Florida. In addition to getting a mountain of peanut butter and jelly, I reached out to the citrus industry and was able to get them to come out with orange juice. After we promoted the notion of having a "back to the basics" lunch, all of the halls in Tallahassee and every government agency emptied out to enjoy a peanut butter and jelly sandwich for lunch.

As it turned out, it was an enormously successful public relations event, so I also decided that we needed to have some kind of a sticker. I came up with a design that included a picture of a peanut, with writing under it that says, "I work for peanuts." I keep some of them around today for laughs, but it has been surprising over the years how many calls I've had from people wanting to use that sticker because they thought that they identified with it. As a matter of fact, at that time Jimmy Carter was running for President and he wanted to have the sticker as well. I decided, maybe rightfully or wrongfully, that this was mine only.

One of my consulting efforts was with the Electro-Optical Systems Division of Xerox in Pasadena. I had a contract with them while they were in competition with IT&T to build the MILES System, which Xerox-EOS ultimately won, and they offered me a job to come out to California to be Co-Program Manager.

What this meant was, while the other guy was more or less the chief engineer, I would be responsible for the budgeting of staff, integrated logistical support, reporting, training, and general program management. It was a huge opportunity and one of those things that I could just not refuse. After all, leaving California to move to Florida was a monumental decision of and by itself, not to mention the impact on my family now that they were rooted in Florida. While all this was going on I was also working as a volunteer on Orlando's Centennial celebration, which happened to coincide with the Bicentennial of the United States. The problem that I was facing was that we were several months short of a series of celebratory events around the American Bicentennial and the Orlando Centennial, most of which (at least on the surface) needed my presence. But because of my new job in California, it created a problem for me being at the right place at the right time. In spite of my responsibilities in both Pasadena and Orlando, the success of the event in Orlando was equally paramount to that of Pasadena, therefore I faced some difficult decisions about where I should be at any given time. Yet here I was, several months short of the very, very important day that we would bring all of our celebrations to a conclusion in Orlando.

Delegating Effectively

Once I had accepted the job in Pasadena, I had to find a way to get back to Orlando as frequently as I could. I had not moved the family while I was in transition and, more importantly, I had to keep things going for the centennial celebration. An army consisting of volunteers was doing the work, and as to reduce my role, I put responsibility for the various events and activities squarely in the hands of the various committee chairs. Instead of my standing on the platform and taking credit every time something happened, I made sure the Committee Chair took it.

With each passing event, you could sense the impact of empowerment, which comes back to a very basic philosophy of delegating the responsibility as well as delegating the authority – it worked like a charm. At the end of the day, everyone knew that I was the Chair of the overall event, but standing there in my stead as a committee chair made all the difference in the world to my hardworking fellow committee chairs.

In the course of moving the Army-Navy game from Philadelphia to the Rose Bowl (which I described in the Prologue), I became involved in the Tournament of Roses in Pasadena, and to this date continue as a lifelong and honorary member of the Tournament of Roses. My success in Pasadena led to my recruitment to the Long Beach Chamber of Commerce for a turnaround assignment.

I've had quite a few jobs in California, including CEO for the Pasadena Chamber of Commerce, which I also previously described, and I eventually became the CEO of the Long Beach Chamber of Commerce. In 1984, under Ronald Reagan's mandate to create a 600-ship Navy, the *U.S.S. Missouri*, the historic battleship on which the Japanese surrendered at the end of World War II, was towed into Long Beach Naval Yard to be re-armed and refurbished. This was a huge undertaking and a huge project, which created considerable pride in the city of Long Beach.

When the Navy decided that it should be unceremoniously re-commissioned and moved to San Francisco, the folks in Long Beach were beside themselves. I was able to reach out to the Chief of Naval Operations, whom I had met during the course of moving the Army-Navy game, and I was able to gain his approval to at least bring the battleship back down to Long Beach for appropriate ceremonies.

This unfortunately did not endear me to San Francisco's Mayor (now Senator), Dianne Feinstein, but I think that at the end of the day everyone won on this one. San Francisco lost nothing and Long Beach regained some well-deserved pride. My job was to take advantage, wherever possible, of news surrounding the *Missouri* to promote business in Long Beach.

There's a sidebar to that. As an Army and Infantry guy, I was interested to learn more about Navy traditions. One of those is that every battleship that is named for a state has a silver service from its namesake. In this case, since the battleship *Missouri* had been decommissioned, its silver service was lodged in the state capitol in Jefferson City. It almost took an act of Congress to dislodge the silver so that it could be returned to the battleship and tradition was served. Incidentally, I learned another interesting piece of trivia about the *Missouri* and its 16-inch guns. They said one of those guns could fire a Volkswagen from Long Beach and drop it into the Rose Bowl in Pasadena.

To this day, I very proudly have in my office some of the planking from the deck of the battleship *Missouri* after it was it was brought back on service.

There is a common thread through all of this, which is don't start your day off by thinking it can't be done. Get rid of some of the simple tasks then attack the bigger ones by breaking them down into bite-sized and more manageable tasks. If need be, treat each day as an objective and approach every day by allocating specific uninterrupted time. I use that uninterrupted time to ensure that those tasks that are of great importance, and were highlighted at the beginning of the day, are dealt with at the end of the day before the corner is turned.

I think budget planning and sales goals fall into that same bag. While you want to assume that you can meet or exceed sales or budget goals, sometimes "it can't be done" – this is a horrible reality to face. I always budgeted conservatively, and also set very aggressive sales goals. By definition, the sales goal cannot equal the budget revenue goal because, in that scenario, you cannot fall short. If you set an aggressive sales goal up beyond your budget or revenue and you fall short, no real harm is done. Obviously you want to meet that more aggressive sales goal, but if you can get between those two numbers, you're golden.

Let me amplify that a tad by saying that in determining your sales goal, you survey your sales team and find out what their goal is. By definition, they will be more conservative. However, if the cumulative sales goals of your team fall short of the goal set by your sales manager, then Houston, you've got a problem. You either don't have enough sales people or you have the wrong sales people.

At the end of the day, you can't afford to have your sales manager, nor any of your other people, stand in front of your desk and tell you it can't be done. Oh, yes, it can be done – if you decide it can.

Chapter 3

Decide to Decide

"Ready, Fire, Aim!"

Nobody would give that command in that order. It doesn't work in combat, and it doesn't work in business, either. "Ready" is the preparation, "Aim" is the decision, and "Fire" is the execution. You cannot put the execution before the decision and expect to succeed – or even survive. The command is "Ready, Aim, Fire!"

You must make the decision before you execute, but in today's fast-paced and highly competitive economy, you can't take too much time on it, and that encourages the "Ready, Fire, Aim!" approach. We've all heard these dodges:

- "I will get back to you...
- "I need more time...
- "I need more information..."

Everybody knows these are codes for "I'm not ready to make a decision," and yet we all keep using them because they are better than no response at all. We may be sincere when we use them, but while we are gathering our information or enjoying our extra time, our competitors are eating our lunch.

If you are in a leadership position in your organization, *you* are the decider, so make your decision. A well-executed bad decision can often prove more successful than doing nothing.

You may risk a great deal in making a decision, but you can reduce the risk by following your gut instinct and gaining experience. While you may not succeed with your decision, there is one thing that is certain: you cannot succeed without deciding. In fact, the failure to make a decision will likely damage your organization by resetting the culture, degrading respect, and undermining loyalty.

For me, making a decision implies making the commitment to realize the decision. The decision is step one in the process of executing it. I have always been that way – after all, I decided at the age of nine that I was going to go to West Point. Just under a decade later I found myself a Cadet at West Point. My point is if you're looking for advice on how to avoid decision-making, you'll have to find a different book.

One Decision Leads to Another

Obviously once I became a Cadet at the US Military Academy I had reset my goals and the next one was to graduate – which happily four years later is exactly what happened.

When I entered West Point, we reported on the 1st of July of 1949. I have already recounted the story of our tour on July 4 in full combat gear, with rifles at port arms, at a double-time march – sometimes you're the decider, and sometimes you're the decided.

Subsequent to graduation, I reported to Fort Benning, Georgia for what was referred to as Basic Infantry Officers training. Fort Benning is the home of the Infantry, and it is also home to a well-known Army landmark: a statue of a Lieutenant with his rifle in his left hand and his outstretched right hand up in the air with the inscription "Follow Me" on its base. Those words are also the motto of the Infantry school.

That statue is a graphic reminder that as a Lieutenant, it will be your duty to lead your soldiers. *You* are the decider. From Infantry School at Fort Benning, I went to Fort Polk, Louisiana to take on my first full-fledged assignment as a Second Lieutenant. This involved an interview with the Regimental Commander – a full Colonel.

I was in my brand new uniform, my brass was all properly shined and properly aligned, and I was good to go. I knocked on the door.

"Enter," said a voice behind the door.

I went through the doorway and moved swiftly toward the desk, halted two paces away, saluted, and rather crisply said, "Good morning, sir. Second Lieutenant Arnhym reports as ordered."

I was secretly pleased with myself for managing the details of this encounter so well.

The Colonel looked at me, gave me a very perfunctory salute back, and said. "Just a damn minute, Lieutenant. I make the decisions around here."

From that moment forward, when I was addressing senior officers I would be very careful with how I described the day. I no longer said, "Good morning" or "Good afternoon," but stuck with the facts. I said "Morning" or "Afternoon" and waited for guidance. I learned the first step in being the decider is to learn how to be the decided.

How to Be the Decided

In another instance, I was assigned to a headquarters in Seoul, Korea sometime after the armistice agreement had been signed, which took place on the 27th of July 1953. That was over 60 years ago. We're still looking at a truce with North and South Koreans facing one another on the 38th parallel and no peace, but don't get me started on tragedies – I can't write that many books.

In Korea, a Colonel I met there told me this story of decisions. His job title was Secretary to the General Staff, and he reported to the Commanding General of 8th Army and US/United Nations Forces Korea. The time had come for the Christmas message to go out to the troops, and the Secretary to the General Staff dutifully put together a draft message for the Four-Star General to sign. It started by stating that the first Christmas was celebrated in a manger.

The Commander in Chief of US Forces in Korea looked at the Colonel rather sternly and asked, "Who says?"

The Secretary to the General Staff said, "Well, Sir. It's written in the Bible."

The General said, "Well, then. Say so."

The message that went out to the troops in South Korea accordingly read as follows: "According to the Bible, the first Christmas was celebrated in a manger."

There are lots of deciders in the Army, and they aren't always the ones you want to be. But when you're the decided, you suck it up and follow orders.

Becoming the Decider

I began to learn to be the decider as Chief of Training at Fort Ord, California – a beautiful place, by the way. During the course of a number of staff meetings, I could not help but note that the delinquency rate on the part of our soldiers had risen, and many were being arrested by the military police in the neighboring communities for drunkenness. This became a hot-button issue at every level. Nothing replaces walking the "four corners," so I decided to follow the soldiers to find out what was going on. I observed that typically the troops would come in from training on the various ranges across Fort Ord, and they would head to the mess hall for dinner, arriving between 5:30 and 5:45.

I have to note that the Army is now probably is a little kinder and gentler, and they now refer to these halls as dining facilities. Call me old-fashioned, but I still think of them as mess halls.

As I continued to watch and observe, I saw that in their desire to get home as soon as possible, the cooks had dinner prepared by 4:30. This meant that the dinner would be on the steam tables for over an hour before the troops would actually arrive.

There aren't many kinds of food that can be kept appetizing on a steam table for an hour, and I assure you that the Army does not serve the few that can. The soldiers would come in, take a look at the food, and head off the base for a burger.

Well, as young soldiers are prone to do, they would stimulate their appetites with a few beers before dinner. By the time they consumed several beers on an empty stomach... you can guess the rest. The military police would find them drunk and disorderly and bring them back to be another statistic at our staff meetings.

There are two ways to deal with a situation like this. You take the predictable way, which is to punish people for misbehavior – that's a very common approach. But often you take the other way, which is an engineering approach. By that I mean you can engineer the situation to discourage misbehavior – take away the reason for the misbehavior, and you will often take away the misbehavior itself.

As the Chief of Training, I jumped into this one. First, I got the approval of the Commanding General to make some new rules for the cooks. I instructed them not to have the food out on the steam tables more than 15 minutes prior to the arrival of our soldiers: the result was dramatic and instant. The food was appealing and the soldiers decided that they would in fact have dinner right there in the mess hall. Once you've eaten in the mess hall, it's natural to look to the amusements nearby rather than to the leave the post. After all, we had a theater and a bowling alley, and the soldiers had their day rooms.

I also suggested that any excess food, and particularly desserts, go to the day room. The day room is a natural gathering place for off-duty soldiers, and the presence of cookies, cake, pie, and sandwiches made it even more attractive. Our arrest statistics changed dramatically, making me a hero to everyone but the cooks.

The lesson in here is pretty clear – sometimes your decisions will not be popular with all of those concerned, but you need to do the best for the majority. In this case, the math was compelling. On one side of the equation were four or five cooks who wanted to get home early. On the other, there were hundreds of soldiers who were likely to go out into the surrounding communities, with all their temptations and opportunities for trouble if the cooks did as they pleased. I chose to endure the anger of the cooks.

Decision making of that sort is obviously a military thing and is inherent in that culture. In combat that sort of decision is a necessity, but training is the key, as it teaches unquestioned response in life and death situations. These kinds of decisions carried over into my civilian careers and I now have a better understanding of the impact of training and good decisions.

The Importance of Execution
I learned a lot of other lessons as the Chief of Training at Fort Ord, one of which was that the better the training and job description, the better the result. What this means is that when people know what they were supposed to do and when they were supposed to do it, you get better results and a better decision-making process. The same is especially true of your staff – if you want well thought out recommendations, then constant training is

a given. If you want top performances from your people on that next-level, repetitive training is a must.

Not all decisions are perfect, however. In the case of an imperfect decision, your best chance of rescue is vigorous and creative execution. Good execution can often compensate for a bad decision. Let me give you a very personal example.

My wife has yet to forgive me for retiring from the Army after a little over 20 years. What drove that decision was pretty basic. I was in a community where I could see a number of retirees who had left the service after 25 or 30 years, and my observation was that too many of them were not very happy in their second careers. They realized that their retired pay alone was not going to allow them to maintain the standard of living to which they had become accustomed.

At the same time, 25 or 30 years downstream and further into their military careers, they were not as marketable as perhaps they were when they were in their mid-40's after 20 years of service. I concluded that if someone came along and offered me a job that I could not refuse, I would then make the shift from military to civilian. If that did not happen, then I was fully prepared to, as we say in the Army, "Continue to march."

As it happened, and by virtue of my exposure within the community, I was offered an opportunity to head a small consulting company doing market research, educational technology, and marketing. The brass ring was probably a little bit bigger than it could have been, at least in my eyes, and I grabbed for it.

Was that the right decision? I don't know, and I will never know. I simply tried to execute it well.

Xerox hired me as a consultant when they were in competition with IT&T to build the training system I described in the previous chapter. When they got the contract, they offered me the job of co-program manager (electro optical systems division in Pasadena, California). My family had become pretty seriously embedded in Florida, particularly our daughters, who eventually opted to go to the University of Florida rather than move to California. Let me tell you, it's a lot easier to survive alienating four or five cooks than alienating a wife and two daughters. Over the course of my professional life, the decision to move to California and work for Xerox turned out well, but I've never been able to figure out whether it was the right or the wrong decision. What I do know is that executed it with all I had.

Life in California
Once I arrived in Pasadena, California and was serving as a Co-Program Manager for Xerox, I found myself heavily engaged on behalf of our company as the point man to the Pasadena Chamber of Commerce. As you have probably surmised as a result of what you read in the Prologue, I was eventually offered the opportunity to become CEO of the Pasadena Chamber of Commerce - an opportunity I accepted. That job led to another career as CEO of various Chambers of Commerce in Pasadena, Long Beach, Palm Springs, and finally in Beverly Hills, California.

It was in Long Beach that I met Buddy Ebsen. We were having drinks and dinner with him and his delightful wife one evening when he mentioned that he was coming up on 60 years in show business. No one, he said, was willing to take on the task of doing a show to showcase those 60 years and bring him the recognition that he had certainly more than earned. Blame it on the wine, but I recklessly said, "So what's so hard about that?"

Well, what happened next should be no surprise. He asked if I could produce a musical to honor his 60 years in show business, and I agreed. Together, we were happily able to put together a musical for him at the Bob Hope Cultural Center in the Palm Springs Area. The show sold out, and I still keep a memento of that experience in my office: a chair that says, "Producer" on it. I'll let you in on a secret: although I was the producer of a successful musical, I cannot carry a tune in a basket. There's an obvious lesson in that, but I'll let you come to your own conclusions.

In the late 1990's, subsequent to similar positions in Pasadena, Long Beach, and Palm Springs, I served as the CEO of the Beverly Hills Chamber of Commerce, which of the various Chambers of Commerce I have served turned out to be the most enjoyable. I met many fascinating and interesting people, not only from the business community, but also from the entertainment industry. I found myself in a very diverse community with innumerable challenges.

I was able to befriend people from all walks of life, all belief systems, and all cultures - and apparently I made my mark. For the longest time after I left Beverly Hills, the newspaper would run a piece on my birthday wishing me a happy birthday. This always inspired a freshet of messages saying, "We thought you had left."

Leaving Beverly Hills was another of those extremely difficult decisions, but with two daughters and their families in Florida, never mind the grandchildren, this was a time for family to outweigh business. The connections I enjoyed in California and especially the Los Angeles area were priceless, but it turns out there are degrees of pricelessness.

It goes without saying that I had the full support of my family in this decision. When I am asked by my California connections why I chose to move, I tell them I had become nostalgic for Vietnam. I missed the heat, the humidity, the snakes, and being shot at: all of those are available in Tampa. In an unusual act of friendship as I was preparing to depart, my friends in Beverly Hills put together a calling tree - every 15 minutes for several hours I got a call from somebody telling me it was not too late to turn back.

Well 2,600 miles plus and several days later I found myself in Tampa, Florida and obviously faced with another decision: shall I do nothing or do something? And what would "something" look like? I decided to decide and that was that I was going to go on a relationship-building rampage in an effort to identify myself in the community and find that perfect next career or opportunity. However, something inside of me said that I was not finished.

I hung out my shingle as a consultant, working on business development and community relations. From there, I continued with my outreach and my relationship building. One day I got a tap on the shoulder and was asked what I thought about becoming a Chair for Vistage, an international organization of some 16,000 executives worldwide.

As a Chairman, I would have an opportunity to put together a group of no less than eight and no more than 16 CEOs. For this group I would act as mentor, facilitator, and coach, helping them to not only grow their businesses but also to grow themselves professionally. As it turned out, this was a perfect fit for me. It was an opportunity for me to give back, to reflect on the lessons that I had learned. It was an opportunity to learn how to ask better questions so I could inspire those in my group to think harder, more out of the box.

Decision-making is tough. Some folks go into a restaurant where there is a buffet and they stall halfway down the line because they don't know what to take.

At West Point, we were taught that there might be a reason, but never an excuse. I would submit that reason is most often a failure to decide. You start everything and finish nothing because you haven't made the commitment that completes the decision. Of all the lessons that I have learned, that is probably the best one.

Chapter 4

Accountability

Look around at a team meeting and ask yourself, "Are they listening?" Their kids can text under the dinner table. Are they any less accomplished? If your employees are "multitasking," and you are simply one of the tasks, can you be sure you are anything more than a distraction? Are your employees fully engaged and are your kids really present at the table?

If outcomes don't always meet expectations, or if you can't always depend on results, chances are good that the people working for you don't fully understand what is expected. It is important to make sure you are heard and understood. Get into the habit of ending every interaction with a question: "Do you have any questions?" At home, a good start is to ask your kids about their day.

In combat, I had to know where members of my command were. Were they doing their jobs and were they fully present? Anything less was unacceptable and potentially fatal in combat. What's different in a highly competitive business environment? The competitive business environment ordinarily lacks land mines and surprise attacks, but it often involves cunning and inexhaustible enemies. You may not need to know where your people

71

are every minute, but you need to ensure they know what is expected of them.

Believe me when I say they hunger for that knowledge. Your employees *want* to be held accountable, and they expect to be rewarded when they exceed performance expectations.

You should get started on developing that accountability before they even come to work for you – with a job description. If you do nothing else in a job interview with a prospective employee, use the job description as a talking paper, and make sure the candidate knows to whom they will report if they get the job. Even if you do that right, there's still a good chance things will fall apart. Clarity requires communication, and often it needs to be communication in person, where both people can give and receive information through all available channels. Email and texting are great for rapidly conveying limited, precise, details. But for anything with nuance, you need face time.

Keeping People on Task

At a minimum, effective management of an employee requires a few tools: the job description, some form of accountability, and the daily huddle. A daily huddle is a simple communication tool that can help you spot problems before they become problems. This can save you from penning the dreaded note: "see me" or "we have to talk."

Here's another thing I've found to be effective: a weekly to-do report. It has to be on my desk every Friday by 4:00 p.m. What I look for in this report is pretty simple. I require a description of the employee's top five priorities for the next week. Then, I need a description of those things that were done and or not done. Finally, I need to know what the employee needs my help or guidance on.

This report gives me the opportunity to ensure that they are on task with respect to their priorities. It says what has been completed and what's not done. I can spot instantly if the things that are not getting done are among the top five priorities, which allows me to get them back on course. Additionally, one look at the bottom of a report tells me if I have failed to adequately communicate or if there is some measure of misunderstanding on their part that was getting in the way of job accomplishment.

The beauty is that I know all of this by every Friday afternoon and I am able to review those reports. By Monday morning, I can focus in on the issues at hand, adjust priorities where necessary, and provide the additional guidance or direction that may be required. But most important factor is that it lets me hold them accountable for their actions. If they are not meeting their priorities, there is a reason for it. If I don't find out the reason, that's a lack of good judgment on my part as well as a signal to them they are being held accountable.

Keeping Yourself on Task

That's how I demand accountability of my people. There's also my own accountability regimen. Twice a day I ask myself two standard questions. At 11:00 a.m., I ask, "Is there's something that I'm doing that somebody else should be doing?" At 4:00 p.m., I ask, "What is it that I came in here to do today that was not done?" Whether I'm holding my employees or myself accountable, these routines will light yellow lights to get my attention. If I deal with yellow lights, I can hope I never have to deal with red ones.

Where do the most difficult problems arise? They are almost always signaled by the assertion we all hate: "It's not my job." When you hear that, there's a misunderstanding that needs correction, and you'll probably want to refer back to the job description. However, you shouldn't get to that if you've been reading the weekly reports carefully.

Frankly, I prefer to give responsibility and authority wherever possible. If there should be limits, set limits, but the key is to make sure they have what they need to do the job. Obviously, the ideal is that somebody who hits a roadblock has the authority to proceed. The worst case is when somebody says, "What should I do?"

I have always found that your best chance of fixing that situation is to you turn the question around: "What do *you* think you should do?" They nearly always have a pretty good idea in mind as to the course of action that should be taken or how they should complete their project or work assignment. The fact is that they're a lot closer to it than you are.

The best situation is for you to be able to respond by saying, "By all means, that's a great idea. Proceed."

If on the other hand their recommendation needs tweaking, then you can modify the approval by saying, "I would suggest you consider making the following changes." Whether you endorse the employee's solution or tweak it, just don't let them give the task back to you. They need to maintain ownership.

If the employee's recommendation is outlandish, then you have to come up with a course of action. This is the worst situation due to the fact that you have tacitly taken ownership of the task and reduced the employee to the role of drone.

Don't Let Your People Delegate Back to You

I vividly recall my time as a CEO of the Beverly Hills Chamber of Commerce, when I was very sensitive and cautious to every written communication that went out the door. I did this because the environment was very critical. I could not afford to have a paper or a letter go out the door that either had errors or misstatement. This is not the ideal role for a CEO, but I became the final inspector of our work. Fortunately, I had the ability to look at any work we were producing and spot a failing, a shortcoming, a mistake, or a misspelling.

To this day, when I run into my former colleagues and those who worked for me they cannot figure out how I did that. They did remember one thing though: I used a dreaded red pen and would mark those communications up and send them back. Be advised that when you do it this way, you are in danger of reducing the employee to a clerk typist. Remember when I said that employees hunger to know what is expected of them? They can read the signs better than you readily imagine.

An employee who has been told to make your edits on the paper they've been working is likely to assume that whatever they next put in front of you will be corrected and sent back so that you can fix it once more. Now you're doing their job again. If you get into that situation, you need to counsel the employee on their work and hold them accountable to do it right the first time. If the person then continues to use you as an editing service, you have to consider the unpleasant alternative of letting them go.

Subsequent to completing the Command and General Staff College at Fort Leavenworth, Kansas, I was assigned to the Pentagon in Washington, D.C. Needless to say the family was beyond happy with the opportunity to be in Washington, D.C. and be able firsthand to be at the seat of government and in a very vibrant environment. We lived in a beautiful community outside of the Beltway. The family absolutely loved it. As for me, I left before dark every morning to get to my job, and I would generally get home after dark. And frankly, I did not see too much of Washington DC.

This was a brand new community, and it was growing to what would eventually be 1500 homes – plus a club, a swimming pool, and an elementary school. I had been asked to serve on the board for our community and ultimately became the President of the Windsor Home Owners Association. This led to the incident in which I learned how to get action out of a committee. It happened like this: I got a letter from the Superintendent of Schools for Fairfax County in Virginia, who offered us the opportunity to come up with a recommendation for a name for the new elementary school. I delegated that responsibility to a committee, and then asked them to go out and come up with a recommendation for a name for the elementary school, then bring it back to an association meeting for approval.

Two months later, I convened the Homeowners Association meeting and asked the committee to come forward with their report. I was fast approaching the deadline that had been given to me by the Superintendent of Schools and therefore clearly needed an answer. The committee had no answer. I don't know if it was because they never met or because they couldn't come to a consensus, but in either case the result was the same: they had no name to recommend. So from the podium, I announced that in my capacity as the President of the Homeowners Association, I was pleased to advise them that in the absence of a report from the committee, I would forward a name for the elementary school. With their approval, I said, the letter going to the superintendent would recommend that the new elementary school be called the Rolfe G. Arnhym Elementary School.

This led to a lot of shuffling of both papers and feet. The committee members disappeared to the back of the building and, about a half an hour later, they came out with their recommendation. Unfortunately, it was not named for me. The name they came up with was Laurel Ridge. Laurel Ridge Elementary School is still the Windsor community's elementary school.

"I'm Doing It as Fast as I Can"
My assignment in the Pentagon was in the Office of the Assistant Chief of Staff for Force Development, located in the Force Accounting Branch.

My office was buried deep within the Pentagon itself. It was on the A circle (the innermost) as opposed to the E circle, which had all of the windows. Shortly after my arrival, my friends and classmates from West Point came by to see where I had been assigned and to welcome me to the Pentagon. They invariably asked, "So Rolfe, what do you do?" My answer, perhaps too facetious, was, "I'm not quite sure, but I'm doing it as fast as I can."

I suppose that uncertainty came from the fact that my job description was a little bit open. Although I was pretty clear about to whom I reported, our mission was to come up with and information system as part of a Uniform Identity Code, which was assigned to all of the parent units of the Army, and further, that there were at least 120+ pieces of information to characterize and better define each one of those units.

Here's an example of the kind of tasks we dealt with: one of the Generals well up the flagpole would give testimony before a House or Senate Armed Services Committee, and a Senator or Congressman might ask, "Why do you need 110 new tanks?"

Well, when they were on the Hill they were of course talking about the budget; there would be a line item in there for the next fiscal year, stating a need for 110 tanks. Usually there was not a lot of explanation attached to it, but in this instance all it took was a member of Congress to ask that rather simple and basic question. The General couldn't be expected to know the reason for every line in the budget, and neither could his staff. That's where we came in. A request would land on my desk to explain why we needed 110 new tanks. This could require an enormous amount of research, which explains why I so seldom arrived home before dark and sometimes stayed at the office late into the night.

The good news is that with the system that we were in the process of putting in place, we could know where each tank was going, what the authorized limits for that particular unit were, and how many they had. Knowing how many they had and how many they needed, we knew how many they were short, exactly where the shortage occurred, and we were able to prioritize it based on mission and location – and that could answer the question. There is a simple lesson here – the two or three star General does not have to have all of the answers, but he does know whom to ask: a Lieutenant Colonel deep in the bowels of the Pentagon... that would be me. What is different about your business or organization?

How to Control Endless Design Changes

That is accountability at the nth degree. It taught me some serious lessons in surrounding myself with good people.

In a previous chapter, I described my consulting in Orlando, Florida where I was a consultant to Xerox when they were in competition with IT&T to build a family of training devices for the Army using laser technology. This system has had a huge impact on training in the Army and in the Marine Corps.

As the Co-Program Manager, most of my responsibilities dealt with budget, training, integrated logistical support, and reports. My other Co was the Chief Engineer on the project, and it was his job to work directly with the various engineers. We had to provide a rather detailed report to the government on a quarterly basis.

This report had to give the status of the design of these various training devices. I learned pretty quickly that the quarterly reports weren't just reports. They touched off discussion and information exchange so that design decisions were second-guessed and those decisions were put back in play; this created havoc with our planning and with our budgeting. This is how and when change orders creep into the equation.

In the design section of the report, I began noting that this is the design as of this date and, unless we hear to the contrary within 30 days, we will assume acceptance and continue on to the next phase. It should be no shock that the report was never read, at least until there was a meeting and those that we were working with within the government were duly surprised and astounded that we had moved on with the design. We made it perfectly clear that the number of dollars that we had proposed and the timeline that we were being held to limited our job. Change orders added time and coast, and it's the birthplace of our overruns.

What occurred next is beyond interesting. Any change that they opted to make in the design was shuttled off to a parallel program and we were therefore able to continue with the project on the timeline and within budget. All the various changes that had come out of these meetings were bundled into an additional add-on contract with a timeline of its own.

Downstream, those changes were either integrated into the design or rejected. The end result – we got a Defense Department Award for on-time and on-budget performance, and the Army got the best possible operating system. Have you ever re-designed your website, or renovated you home? Why don't we have the door over there instead of as planned? Does this sound familiar?

What CEOs Want to Be Accountable for

My most recently lesson in accountability came from my work with Vistage, where I serve as a chair of three groups. Vistage is an international organization of over 16,000 executives worldwide and, as a chair, I'm one of about 850 around the world that have any number of groups that can number from one to four. A group can have as few as eight members and, generally speaking, no more than 18. They are organized around the concept of the size of a company and level of leadership, with CEOs and Presidents of companies are in one group, key leaders in another, and finally the first line of direct reports and entrepreneurs in another.

A recent survey made it perfectly clear that the most important experience to those members, and their most desired return on their investment of time and dollars, was to be held accountable. I saw those results and was a little bit perplexed, and so I went back to my groups and said, "Very cool, folks. I understand you want to be accountable. Can you tell me what you want to be held accountable for?" I got a lot of blank looks.

I did not let them off the hook, however. As a part of a goals matrix that I maintain, there is a column that says, "Hold me accountable for," and within that column I enter the accountability each member wants. Some of the answers are pretty interesting:

- "Make sure that I make a prompt and good decisions."
- "Make certain I improve my communication skills so that I interact more with my people."
- "I just don't have a good and full understanding of a financial report, and I've got to have a better understanding of a financial reporting systems."

That's just a brief sample. There are many more.

The bottom line is that there is a set of givens and now I'm going to give you five bullets.

- Hire employees you can depend on. Fire those that you can't.
- Have a defined accountability model and clear expectations.
- Communicate.
- Create a culture of being fully present. No playing with their IT toys in a meeting.
- Without accountability and a team you can depend on, you will fail as a leader.

With that said, one of the major reasons why you will more often than not start everything and finish nothing is because you either failed to hold somebody accountable or worse, you didn't hold yourself accountable.

Chapter 5

Delegation

"It's easier if I do it."

I'm sure you've heard that before. I know I have, but I can't remember a time when it was easier – if I cut the lawn or cleaned the pool, or got frustrated putting up the Christmas lights, somehow it was never easier when I did it.

Before you say, "It's easier if I do it," stop and think a moment. Is it easier if you make the coffee in the office? It's probably a wonderful gesture, but try it. You'll find after a while, you're the official coffee maker.

Is it easier if you fix the copier? If so, it's probably a direct result of your involvement in ordering the machine to begin with, so that you are the only one in the office who knows how to fix it.

For several years now, everyone in business management has been streamlining in an effort to reduce overhead and obviously personnel costs. This streamlining has necessarily caused casualties, and one of those casualties has been the Administrative Assistant, sometimes known as the Executive Assistant and once called the Secretary.

Out of necessity, many business owners, CEOs, and company presidents eliminated that position, assuming technology and simplified procedures would allow them to take over the assistant's tasks themselves. We've all had the opportunities to see if it was indeed easier if we made and confirmed our own appointments, sorted our mail, dealt with our email and text messages, made our own travel plans, set up meetings, and produced handouts for them. How has that worked out for you?

Assuming that the person whose position was eliminated worked a full eight-hour day, those eight hours have been added to your "eight" (did somebody say nine, ten, or 11?) hours. How effective are you now that you work a 16- or 19-hour day? Is it still easier if you do it yourself?

When I moved the Army-Navy game, the logistics were almost overwhelming, and they had to be tackled even while I was still in negotiations to get the game moved. In parallel with my meetings, pitches, and negotiations, there was television and newspaper coverage to be managed, food and housing for 10,000 Cadets and Midshipmen to be planned, rehearsal space and facilities to be lined up for the bands, printing of programs and collateral materials, transporting of mascots to be arranged, traffic control to be planned with the police and city authorities, security arrangements to be made with the police, events and festivities to be organized, data processing to be mobilized, and – above all – fundraising conducted to finance it. If I had not had an army of volunteers to whom I could delegate those thousands of tasks, the 1983 Army-Navy game would have been stuck in Philadelphia.

Everybody is Behind in Their Work

I think if you're honest, you will admit that at the end of the day, a lot of your tasks are just not completed. I hope you can carry over a few to the next day, where they will bump other tasks, until you are in a permanent state of behind on your work. I imagine that's the *best* I can hope for you. I think we've all probably been a little bit behind at least since there have been workplaces. But I don't think it has ever been like it is today. We have every convenience and every productivity tool, and yet the world is a welter of unreturned phone calls, late deliveries, and missed deadlines. Smart people no longer make promises for deliveries, and when they are forced to, they pad the schedule by adding a day for every day they expect the job to take.

No wonder a Google search on "time management" returns over 500 million hits. No wonder time management workshops are a booming business. No wonder *Getting Things Done* is the number seven best-selling book in the "Mental Health" category at Amazon.

I once heard a speaker take pride in having over 250 items dispersed over various online files on his iPhone. Now there's a man who knows how to *start* tasks.

Frankly, I pushed his buttons a little bit. I pointed out that he had all of those messages or all of those reminders for tasks that needed to be done neatly tucked away in a number of files totally hidden from view so it wouldn't drive him crazy. However, when I challenged him to open up some of those files, he was in shock because he realized that while he was very fastidious about recording the things that he had to do, he wasn't getting it done.

At the end of the day... Wait a minute. I know I use this expression "at the end of the day" a lot, but when is the end of the day? Modern work is 24/7. There is no end of the day. OK. I'll try not to write it for the rest of the book. How do we reconcile the 24/7 workplace with the now 30-hour work week? With the rise of flextime and job-sharing, sometimes we assign one job to two employees, each working 20 hours. Then, however, we have to live with discontinuities and more logistical problems. Jobs don't get completed when they should. What happened to the 40-hour workweek, where CEOs were working 50 or 60 hours to get the job done as to finish what they started?

In the world of working 24/7, it is not uncommon for someone to send a message during the early morning hours when most of us are sleeping. If you are one of those, you have probably already learned you cannot ask two questions in a message, because you're only going to get one answer. As I said previously, nobody scrolls after 2:00 a.m.

The Right People in the Right Jobs

In the book *Good to Great,* Jim Collins argues that you need to get the right people on the bus. The right people are disciplined people who think and work in a disciplined way. If you don't have those people in the right jobs, you're not going to achieve greatness. But there's another dimension beyond having good people in the right jobs, and that's ensuring they are free to do those jobs. Sometimes that means riding them in unpleasant ways.

In Vietnam, I worked out of a firebase in the jungle. A firebase essentially was a circular area within which you position your forces. On a daily basis, your forces moved out from the circle to conduct search and destroy operations.

In this particular case, it was a Battalion – about 850 personnel. Clearly I had the right people in the right place to get the job done. But almost all fire bases had the right people in the right jobs, and there were still far too many overrun in the middle of the night by the Viet Cong or North Vietnamese soldiers. What happened to the right people?

We would always have at least two people on each shift position, so one could sleep and the other one could keep watch. Unfortunately, that was not always the case. My instructions all the way down the line were to continue to check on your people and to make sure that they are awake and doing their jobs.

Frankly, I took it upon myself to ensure that my orders were instructed down to the last man. Was this a lack of trust or micromanaging? Maybe so, but I felt I needed to keep it up until my subordinate commanders finally got the idea that they were being held accountable, and that they needed to be holding their people accountable. Sometimes you need to micromanage until the message is received. You don't take any chances in combat, but maybe you feel you can take chances in your business. If so, just remember that some of your competitors may be combat-trained.

The point of the combat story is that if conditions require you to micromanage (and I would argue the life-and-death conditions of combat qualify), go ahead and micromanage. Be sure to know why you're doing it, and stop as soon as you can. Get the right people in the right jobs, and then let them do those jobs, but never assume it is being done.

Your Main Job: Grow Your People

Clearly in a small company, managers wear many hats. But as your company grows, and you add that first line of direct reports, you must put trust and confidence in your subordinates and let them do the job as opposed to you jumping in and doing it yourself. The temptation for the CEO to do the work of the marketing or sales VPs can be very strong, but your VPs cannot grow in their jobs if you're always doing their jobs.

Here is a perfect example: every business has to decide what dollar level of expenses doesn't require the approval of the CEO. In small businesses, the founder or CEO usually feels tremendous pressure to keep and need this approval to him or herself. In every business in which I have been CEO, however, I have authorized my CFO to sign off on any check of $500 or less. I felt I could do this because I have always hired competent, trustworthy CFOs. This accomplishes two things: 1) it dramatically reduces the number of checks sitting in my IN tray waiting for my signature, making my work more focused and efficient, and 2) it sends a clear message to the CFO that I have his or her back, meaning more confident decisions and more freedom of action.

Let me explain it terms of sports. Everybody loves sports metaphors, right?

Clearly the football quarterback doesn't win games alone - he depends on every member of that football team to make it happen. As a tennis player, I can tell you that when I am playing doubles, I rely on my partner to backstop me and to get those shots that either go over my head or are on his side of the court.

Professional golfers have a team behind them, race drivers have a team supporting them, and teams or task forces do most of the work in your business as well.

Teams and task forces not only create a more supportive environment, but also tend to hold each other accountable. This helps ensure that tasks don't go uncompleted or it helps ensure the job gets done.

I also found that cross training was an imperative, particularly to cover for when someone called in sick or there was a conflict that meant a key member of the team or a task force was not available.

Have you ever noticed that when you have an office party to celebrate an anniversary or a birthday, someone grabs a piece of cake and retreats to their own desk? This could be a sign of dedication to the job, but it isn't a sign of dedication to the team. Keep an eye out for the person who refuses to participate – it could be a warning that other members of the team will ultimately be burdened with this person's work.

The Annual Business Plan
Here is where "It's easier if I do it" is the most rampant: the annual business plan. I have seen too many CEOs and company presidents prepare a plan, establish the goals and objectives, and then take it to a strategic planning session.

Members of the leadership team are very attentive to this plan and no doubt take copious notes, because they didn't have input into this process. How committed will they be to implementing the plan if they have no ownership? It may take a lot of effort and time to involve the members of the leadership team in developing the plan, but it's worth it for you to play the role of facilitator rather than dictator.

There's considerable merit to having an outside facilitator, due to the fact that he or she will see things that you do not but, frankly, it burned up a lot of energy and time on my part just getting them up to speed. Obviously, you can save some of this effort by having the same person come back year after year. This gives them a better grasp of your organizational structure in your "SWOT" – your strengths, weaknesses, opportunities, and threats.

Doing it yourself is always an option, and here's how I've done it: working with my leadership team, we developed an agenda, expectations of each member of that leadership team, and the role that they would be playing during the course of the strategic planning session. The most important part of any strategic planning session should be bottom-up input.

I believe there is no such thing as a bad idea, so what we would typically do is everyone was required to play a role in terms of bringing in some new ideas, some new business niche, and some concept that could improve how we went to market.

Because there is no such thing as a bad idea, every idea went up on the wall. However, some ideas are better than others, so we would rank them. One thing to keep in mind is that it is important to recognize that every idea has its own time; an idea might be good, but it's just not the right time for it, and this may mean carrying it over to another year. Here's how we kept the approach positive: every player had to explain how to make the idea happen, not why it could not.

As the CEO, I was the only naysayer. This created a very interesting dynamic, and you could feel the energy level in the room literally rise because everyone became animated. They were literally knocking themselves out trying to figure out how to make that idea work.

Needless to say, the idea's original proponent was gratified and felt encouraged to continue to bring ideas to these meetings and frankly to our staff meetings. "It's easier if I do it" is almost always counterproductive, but when it comes to bringing ideas into the organization, it is the worst possible approach. As the owner and CEO, if you are the only one coming in with ideas, you might as well build a wall around the organization because you'll never grow beyond what you are now.

"It's easier if I do it." No, it isn't – it may take time and effort to involve others, but ultimately they are time and effort worth investing. It's an investment in the growth of your organization's people. If they don't grow, the organization won't grow. Therefore, be sure to not only delegate tasks, but also delegate the authority, the resources, and the responsibility that go with them as well. In addition to this, make sure to delegate decision-making – if all the decision-making rests in your hands, then the organization is stifled and not a great deal is going to be done by the end of the day or week or month.

I may be the starter, but I don't always have to be the finisher. When I reduced the incident reports at Fort Ord by ensuring the soldiers' dinners were optimum serving temperature when they arrived, it was enough for me to create the plan. I didn't have to cook the food, too. And, believe me, the soldiers were better off that I didn't. I don't know how to cook for large groups of men, and if I'd decided it was easier for me to do it myself, we would have had higher incident reports rather than lower.

Chapter 6

Working with People

More often than not, the reason that you find yourself starting everything and finishing nothing is because of people. You haven't delegated some of the more time consuming tasks either to a member of your staff or to your executive assistant.

Many CEOs believe they have leadership teams, when all they have are direct reports – two to three people, or even five to eight, who represent the various disciplines needed by a modern organization: sales, marketing, IT, finance, whatever. Your span of control is more often than not driven by the size of the organization and the need to have the various disciplines covered. Too many CEOs regard these direct reports as individuals to whom they give tasks with the expectations that jobs get done. Too often and unfortunately, these direct reports are given responsibility without authority.

On the other hand, in the ideal scenario, these direct reports form a leadership team: a number of people that can function as a group, all focused on organizational goals. This group also provides you with recommendations and input based on the simple fact that they are usually closer to the problem than you are yourself.

You cannot turn your direct reports into a team without first delegating to them the authority to do their individual jobs. If you are constantly second-guessing them or they must return to you after each step for approval to embark on the next one, they will never be team members. They will always be minions and their lack of autonomy will set a limit to your effectiveness.

As I previously stated, some small companies require the CEO's approval for every check over $1,000, or even for every one over $500. As the company grows, the ever-present stack of requests on the CEO's desk is higher and higher. This, by definition, is a wasteful process, and more often than not, is something that can and should be done at a lower level. Soon the CEO is spending a major portion of his or her day signing requests. This doesn't lead to better decision making, for as the company grows, the CEO is further removed from the work and understands less and less the import of each request. The CEO is a bottleneck in organizational workflow. If something goes wrong, it is magnified and multiplied by the need to involve the CEO – precious hours or even days are lost when an astute vice president or CFO could have corrected the problem.

I have observed CEOs who cannot sit through a meeting of any length, breaks aside, who feel the need to check on their direct reports constantly. If they cannot be trusted or do not have the authority, something is very wrong.

The effective organization is one in which the CEO understands the necessity for quick, responsive, and fast decision-making in a very mobile environment. The CEO, who spends very little time on middle-level decisions and almost none on day-to-day matters, spends his or her time gaining an understanding of the organization and his or her direct reports. The CEO has got to know each of these direct reports, their capabilities, their shortcomings, their proficiencies, and even how they will respond to different situations. Working with people is not a science – it's an art.

Culture Counts

In the military, it is very well understood that leadership and command are all about knowing the people who work for you. As a Lieutenant, one of my first responsibilities was to take command of 41 soldiers. Although I had four squad leaders and a Platoon Sergeant, I was expected to know every one of those 41 soldiers so that I could identify them by the back of their neck, know exactly what they were going to do, when they were going to do it, and how they were going to do it.

They also understand delegation in the military. At Fort Riley, Kansas I found myself as the Aide-de-Camp, a position authorized for general officers, and these individuals serve in a number of capacities, primarily as a special assistant executing some of the tasks that would otherwise distract from the General's broader responsibilities. In my case, I was working for a two-star General who was commanding Fort Riley, Kansas and the 10th Mountain Division. In addition to military responsibilities, it was his responsibility to forge a strong link between the military population at Fort Riley and the two nearby communities of Junction City and Manhattan, Kansas.

I always accompanied him on those visits to the local community and in particular, to special events and activities that he was invited to attend. Quite often, my role was simply to take notes when someone from the civilian community asked for some assistance in a matter that impacted on both the civilian and the military communities. This might be a Mayor or a member of County Commission or some business leader. I would take copious notes, and then back at the office I would take care of whatever details were involved and ensure that the appropriate individuals were called upon to follow up. The General could focus on larger matters that way.

Some years later, I had a job at the Electro-Optical Systems division of Xerox in Pasadena, California. As I wrote in a previous chapter, we were charged with developing laser technology devices for training and I was the Co-Program Manager. Shortly after I arrived at the plant in Pasadena, California my boss, the head of the Department of Engineering, called me in.

"Arnhym," he said, "what are you doing?"

I was a little puzzled. "What do you mean, what am I doing?"

"You're driving these guys crazy," he said.

"I don't understand," I said.

"When you come in in the morning on your way to your desk, you're greeting everybody with a salutation good morning."

I was astounded.

"You're driving them crazy," he said again. "They don't want to be talked to. They just simply want to get from their car to their desk and bury themselves in their work."

Obviously, I didn't understand the people. In the military, if a junior approached a senior, it was expected they would salute and say either "Good morning" or "Good afternoon." I was in a new culture, and I had to learn it in a hurry.

Working with People

When I was a member of the Rotary Club in Pasadena, California, they had a tradition that is a little different than what I was used to. If someone had a birthday, they would be fined $100 and the President of the club would ask the birthday person to say something. One time, the President reached out to an individual who was the President of a local mortuary and asked him if he would care to say anything since it was his birthday and he was going to be fined $100.

"No, I have nothing to say," said the Mortuary President.

The President of the club kept asking him over and over again and still there was no answer.

Finally, a little bit exasperated, the President of the club said, "Why don't you tell us what is it you like about your work?"

"It's a chance to work with people," said the Mortuary President.

I have often remembered that answer when conducting job interviews. In a job interview, you want to get a sense of a candidate's skill set or proficiency, areas where they are strong, and areas where they are weak. You have no way to get this information except by asking questions. I have often brought interviews to a close by saying, "Why don't you tell me about something that you feel that you do very well."

Too often, the answer is, "I guess I enjoy working with people."

I usually reply, "So do morticians."

"Working with people," means different things to different people. But in my way of thinking, you can't work effectively with people unless you transcend superficialities.

As the CEO of the Beverly Hills Chamber of Commerce, I found myself working with Republicans, Democrats, and businessmen and women of every faith. From my perspective, it was totally seamless. I didn't care what label they might carry in other circles; I was there to represent the business community and to ensure that business was strong and growing. To me, everything else was superficial.

I reached out to every group, and when I finally left the Beverly Hills Chamber of Commerce and was preparing to move to California, not only was I asked to serve on the nominating committee for my successor, but also I received awards from every one of the various groups acknowledging what I had done to create a partnership environment. I had no problem reaching out to the opposite political party, whether in the State legislature or in a Congressional office. I didn't have an issue connecting with members of different religious communities either. My goal was to be able to establish relationships with all kinds of people from all different backgrounds no matter what.

The Perils of Prejudice

While I was in Beverly Hills, we picked up on the fact that a number of our residents were not shopping in Beverly Hills. We presumed this was due to cost – that that Mercedes-Benz in Beverly Hills was going to be more expensive than that Mercedes across the street in Los Angeles. We then decided to conduct a study utilizing graduate students from the business school at UCLA, and what we found out was that the issue was not price.

The issue was customer service. There's a telling scene in the movie *Pretty Woman,* in which Julia Roberts's character is trying to buy clothes to give her an appearance less likely to embarrass tycoon Richard Gere when she's with him. But in every shop she enters, the staff sense immediately that she's a prostitute and none of them will give her the time of day. That scene is an authentic portrayal of what we had to deal with - most people default to dealing with the superficial aspects of others.

As in the situation with Julia Roberts, where image and perception tend to intersect, one of the best examples of being misread occurred to me while I was living in the city of Claremont, home to six small colleges and universities. A number of us had opted as a group to go to the theater. As we headed to our seats subsequent to the break, one of my friends (just out of a lark) handed me his program and asked if I would sign it. So, I was standing in the aisle signing his program, and somebody in the aisle behind me saw what I was doing and asked me to sign their program.

Inexplicably, this started a rush, and suddenly I found myself signing 25 or 30 programs. As the lights began to dim and it was time for me to head towards my seat, the audience stood and applauded me. They had no idea who I was – they simply assumed that I must be a celebrity. Why else would someone be coming up to me for an autograph? The lesson here is fairly simple: you project multiple images and you can never tell what anybody is thinking, or is likely to do based on the strength alone of either how you are dressed or how you carry yourself.

From Gold to Platinum

As a result of the study, and after understanding the real issue, I conducted a workshop on customer service (that you will read about later) and when confronted by a CNN TV reporter with the question of whether or not we were dissatisfied with the level of customer service in Beverly Hills. I said, "No, we were just simply trying to get from gold to the platinum level." This is another way of saying that in working with people the imperative is to push them to their maximum capacity and work to get the best out of them. Relating to your customers is one thing, and relating to your people is another.

Studies have shown that 71 percent of those who leave their job cite interpersonal relationships as the reason. This shows important it is to listen to your people, to walk the four corners, to be alert for conflict, to listen and communicate with people, and to know what to expect from them.

I've always made it a point when I walk into somebody's office to look around and spot objects in that office that tells me that individual has a story to tell. I know I can hear the story just by asking them to tell it. This is true whether I'm visiting a member of my team, a subordinate, a colleague, a client, or particularly a prospective client. I break down barriers by hearing people's stories. Elsewhere in this book, I've mentioned listening as the great skill of leadership. You should exercise it constantly. It is so easy to get a person talking in their office, as a normal person's workspace is crammed with clues to ask about: diplomas, certificates, group photos, and trophies, or even knick-knacks. The key to working with people is the ability to quickly sense those things in which they take pride. Engage them in a conversation about this and you will have an instant friend.

Take People as They Are

People are people; they expect you to look them straight in the eye. People today are impatient. Only in today's world could you imagine somebody pacing in front of the microwave. Why? Because today's world is 24/7 - we have email, text, and phone, and we have learned to communicate whenever the spirit moves us and to expect an immediate answer. Incidentally, I have found that that if I exchange two successive messages, whether by text or email, I can save myself a lot of additional effort by picking up the phone. Frankly, typing has never been my strong suit – I've been happier on a hand grenade range than in front of a keyboard.

I do, however, have a pet peeve, and that's people who do not respond to email messages, or to text messages, or only to that part of the message that is in the frame in front of them, all due to the fact that they haven't scrolled all the way down. More often than not, I find it necessary to text a message back or email back and say, "Did you see the rest of my message?" I hate that. What I hate even more are people who don't respond to phone calls or don't

RSVP until the last minute. I think a special circle of Hell should be reserved for those who get on the calendar weeks in advance, and when you reach out to confirm, they tell you they've got a conflict. What happened? Am I less important than the other person or did I suddenly become of lesser priority? And frankly, when were they going to share that piece of information with me? When I showed up and they weren't there?

I have to ask myself if these are people that I really want to be doing business with. Sometimes you have no choice and have to do business with them, so you've just got to learn how to work with these people. This is one of the areas where a considerable amount of time is wasted, and you can't get done the tasks that you had intended to do because you're doubling back trying to establish another meeting time, which will probably go back and forth multiple times before you find a time that works for both of you. It is safe to say that I'm sure you could write your own book on rude people.

One of my favorite stories is when I was a member of the California-Nevada Super Speed Train Commission. We had the opportunity to take a technology trip to Europe to visit both Germany and France, where there were examples of high-speed rail. Our flight took off from Los Angeles International Airport late in the afternoon. It was a Lufthansa flight, and our flight path was going to take us the polar route. I was happily seated on the left side in business class. The sun was slow to set through drinks and dinner and dessert. Finally, we were finished with the meal service when the German flight attendant announced that they were getting ready to show the movie. It's too bad I can't reproduce his accent on this page, but you can imagine it for yourself. He admonished everyone to please put his or her shades down in preparation for the movie to begin – this was in the days before seats had individual screens. There happened to be a genius sitting in front of me who was buried in his book with his shade still up. Obviously, he could have used his light, and this would not have been a disturbance, but the setting sun cast a shadow across the screen, making it difficult to view the movie.

The flight attendant went over to this gentleman, reached across him and with a couple of fingers slid the shade down and rather empathically said, "Shades down, we are now showing the movie." He probably thought that the flight attendant was rude, that everybody else on the plane was rude, but that's life. You have to adjust to people who may not be in total concurrence with the way you're thinking or behaving.

The Incredible Shrinking Customer Base

Working with people is never easy. Gaining their support, their loyalty, and their commitment is crucial. That rude person that was seated in front of you on a plane could easily be your next client. If you don't believe me, let me tell you about a flight I had in which a gentleman sitting next to me who was completely buried in his book. It struck me that he probably did not want to be bothered, and so for quite a while I left him totally alone. The dinner service offered an opportunity for a break, which is when I leaned over and asked him to tell me a little bit about himself and where he was going. It turned out that he was from Perth, Australia, was doing business in the United States, and was in fact living and working in the same city where I was located. Ironically, he ultimately became a client.

As the CEO of the Palm Springs Chamber of Commerce, I found myself faced with a serious issue one year: visitors were not coming to Palm Springs. If you're in Los Angeles, you're two hours from the mountains, two hours from the desert, and certainly less than two hours from the beach. There were just too many choices. If the weather is good on the beach, then people are not going to come to the desert. If there's snow, they'll go to the mountains. The question was how do you motivate people to come to the desert when they have so many choices? So, I did something really "out of the box." On the anniversary of Paul Revere's ride in mid-April, I rented a horse, put on a three-cornered hat, got a lantern, and rode down Palm Canyon Drive yelling, "The tourists are coming!" It sounds absurd, but the media covered it. It hit the Los Angeles market, and the people came. If you have a good idea of how people might respond, don't ever worry about feeling silly putting on a costume and getting on a horse.

All of us know the importance of knowing people. It gets us referrals, tickets to sporting events, the theatre, in to see people protected by gatekeepers, and the list goes on. It essentially gets us in the door. How many of us like to know the key person at our favorite restaurant so we can get the best table and the best service? I had such an entry to a very exclusive restaurant in Los Angeles. This place had started by serving chili out a window to members of the entertainment community. Gradually, it became a place to have a great meal and see important people. I had an amazing experience myself. However, I did note that those coming in for the first time were placed in less favorable locations. The staff knew most of the clientele, and their regular customers all had their favorite tables. One day I read in the *LA Times* that they were closing. How could this happen to one of the city's most exclusive restaurants? The answer is simple – one by one, their favorite clients retired or moved to the desert and they were gradually losing their base.

As a result of their less than favorable treatment, first-time customers did not return to the restaurant. The owners had become complacent, as they were always full and busy. They apparently didn't notice that, little by little, their base was shrinking. When it caught up to them, they were forced to close. The simple lesson learned is that "working with people" includes good customer service to *all* customers, because one day they will be your favored customers as your current favored customers fade away.

It was in Palm Springs that I got a lesson in the power of humor. Our office got a call from *Good Morning America*, and they wanted me to report the weather on the show from Palm Springs. As it turned out, the site that they had in mind was in Rancho Mirage and not really in Palm Springs. I have always tried not to worry about small details, but it did create a little bit of anxiety with some of my cohorts down valley. *Good Morning America* wanted to send an advance team out to check out the locations for the filming, and we were very prompt to make the necessary arrangements for them. I said that I would be happy to take them to lunch after they finished their visit of potential locations. There is a really neat restaurant called Melvyn's at the foot of Ramon Drive, which runs right up against the mountain, and is a watering hole for the rich and famous when they visit Palm Springs. Their maître d' in particular was very sensitized to his clientele and knew exactly how to respond when they were visiting for a meal. I had become close to Brian, and we understood each other very, very well. When I learned that the *Good Morning America* team was going to be in Palm Springs I gave him a call and said, "I tried to make a reservation for lunch at IHOP but they were full, and I figured that the next best answer would be if l brought them to your restaurant for lunch." We got there and of course, the restaurant was crowded, but he had set aside a table for us. When we sat down, we were given IHOP menus – Brian had gone down to IHOP, grabbed some of their menus, and inserted the Melvyn's menu inside of the IHOP menu. The folks from *Good Morning America* were very impressed with his sense of humor, my sense of humor, and the fact that we knew how to get along with each other and make good things happen.

My point here is pretty simple - more often than not a good sense of humor can get you a long way in trying to improve how you work with other people. Too often we tend to have an inflated opinion of ourselves, which can inhibit our ability to work with people.

I recall being in a car with three local business leaders when the opening of Disney World was about to make a dramatic change on the city of Orlando. We were on our way out to a visit with one of the Senior Vice Presidents from Disney who was charged with not only finalizing the negotiations for the acquisition of the necessary land, but to get the construction phase underway and to integrate their efforts with those of the community.

The four of us were trying to come up with the name of an individual that could best be the liaison from the City of Orlando to Disney World. While we were throwing names all over the place, one of the others in the car remarked, "You know, as we speak, there is a meeting in somebody's living room right here in Orlando, where a group of ladies are trying to decide who the den mother should be for the wolf patrol of a local Cub Scout pack." It was a funny remark, given the situation, but it was also a reminder that at every level, decisions are being made about leadership. In every case, careful attention is given to the leadership skills of that person, but in particular their ability to work with others.

Over the course of multiple careers, I have learned the importance of being alert to opportunities to bring people together and to create a healthy and harmonious environment where teamwork is a given, and no challenge is too great. The bottom line is that if you're going to get your task done and if you're going to avoid a scenario where you start everything and finish nothing, then working with people is an imperative. All business professionals can read numbers, but few can understand and read people.

Today's CEO leads an isolated life. He or she makes decisions that are the responsibility of no one else. Sometimes these decisions can be undermined by personal relationships, so the conscientious CEO tries to avoid those relationships. But isolation in this case is metaphorical, not physical – you cannot hide behind a closed door. As the CEO, you work through other people, and that means knowing them, appreciating them, and appealing to the best that is in them. As a CEO, you are more than a decision maker – you're a team builder.

People come in all sizes and shapes. The good news is that there are people that light up the room and bring energy. There are others who suck the air out. In my Vistage CEO Group meetings, I have seen both ends of this spectrum. While at times I feel like I am herding cats, this is where leadership skills come into play, creating a fine mix of diplomacy and finding a way to engage that individual who brings nothing. Look carefully around the room during a staff meeting and see if you don't have the person I am talking about. In a sense, you have the right person on the bus (good to great) but they may not be in the right seat (out of their comfort zone) or may be facing the wrong direction (culture and buy in).

Melting an Ice Queen and the Mayor of Moscow

Part of dealing with people is being caught off guard. Someone will say or do something that catches you unready or not knowing what to do next. Two instances pop into my mind, both taking place when I was the CEO of the Beverley Hills Chamber of Commerce. I got a call from the office of the Mayor of Moscow (Russia, and not Idaho). It's a long story, but it seems that my picture and an article on me had appeared in a Moscow newspaper. The bottom line is that for a foreign dignitary to get a visa to visit the US they need an invitation. As I was about to be said "inviter," I gave it a quick thought and said yes. This certainly speaks to "Ready, fire – aim!" It struck me that this could be a huge PR event for Beverley Hills and, of course, I had to explain all of this to my Board as well as the City Council. They were aghast, but went along with it. In the weeks leading up to the visit, more phone calls took place to include "Can the Mayor bring a few business and government associates?" I thought to myself, "A few men and another car? No big deal." This unfortunately morphed into an AEROFLOT – a special flight with over 200 Russians heading to Beverley Hills. This took the visit to a whole new level and was not a meeting with a direct link to Moscow.

Now, here is where the melting of the ice queen began. The Russians had sent a TV crew from one of their leading TV stations, so we provided a downlink so that the meetings and events taking place in Beverly Hills could be seen concurrently in Moscow. As it turned out, I was about to be interviewed by their anchor – a drop-dead gorgeous blonde. We were inches apart as we were testing the microphone and the volume and so forth. She may as well have been made of ice, but I could not stop myself – I looked at her straight in the eye and said, "Would you like to defect?" The result was marvelous: she broke out in a big smile, and we were buddies. I probably ended up having more fun with this interview than the Mayor of Moscow had at the Playboy Mansion.

In the second situation, we were getting complaints from merchants of Beverley Hills saying that residents were not buying goods and services in the city. The perception was that Mercedes at the Mercedes of Beverley Hills was more expensive than the one across the city line and in Los Angeles. By virtue of the relationship we had with the College of Business at UCLA, we put an MBA student group on the project to determine how to change the "perception." What we learned was that the issue was really about customer service. Sound familiar? This takes us back to *Pretty Woman*. We decided, as a result of these findings, to conduct a workshop on customer service for all front-end personnel of stores, hotels, restaurants and the like. Another issue arose when we attempted to get the Rodeo Drive folks in the room. It finally came together and I was headed to the podium to welcome over 200 attendees, when through the doors came a CNN TV crew, lights on and headed for me. The reporter looked at me and said, "We understand that you are doing a workshop on customer service for front-line personnel." I, of course, said yes. They then said, "We therefore assume that you are dissatisfied with the customer service in Beverley Hills!" My brain turned to sludge out of nowhere and I replied, "No, we are just trying to get from gold to PLATINUM!" I have no idea where that came from, but the lights went out and they were gone. How many times have you been caught off guard and how did you react? There is no class, per se, on quick thinking but I would submit that as a CEO, you have to add that arrow to your quiver.

Chapter 7

In Conclusion...

"In conclusion..."

How did those become the two most beautiful words in the English language? Just think about how many years of your life you have used enduring the 30 to 90 minutes' worth of words leading up to them. Your sore bottom, your numbed brain, your heavy eyelids sing hymns of gratitude when they hear "In conclusion..."

Over the course of multiple careers, I have had the privilege of making presentations to Boards of Directors, City Councils, County Commissions, State Legislative bodies, State Houses and Senate, and in one instance before the Civil Works Committee of the U.S. House of Representatives. During the course of a military career, I've done innumerable briefings at various levels as well. For every presentation I have made, I simply stood up there and I said, "Good morning" or "Good afternoon" and then followed with, "In conclusion..." and went on to tell them exactly what I was going to tell them, looked them straight in the eye and said, "Good afternoon and thank you very much." I have never known this approach to work anything less than perfectly.

I found that in those very, very brief moments it would be pretty clear and self-evident that they got my message. Whether it was a request, whether it was a recommendation, it didn't make a lot of difference – but I got right to the point at the very, very beginning.

If there was any doubt in their minds or if I got a quizzical look, or if somebody just was shaking their head, then I knew that I had more work to do. I would go on with my presentation until I had provided them with enough information to get it. Then, I would once again say, "In conclusion..." and give them the conclusion again.

As I look back on my various careers, I like to think about the person-years I have saved our economy (not to mention people's own lives) by providing my conclusion first.

Getting to the Point

In our senior year as a Cadet at West Point, one of our requirements in senior English was to do a book review. The idea was that we were to go to the library, a place that I hated with a passion, and there we would find that several were shelves set aside with various worthy writers chosen by the English department. Our mission simply put was to grab one of those books, read it, and provide a written review.

I was in a bit of a hurry because I was uncomfortable in the library, when I spotted the name of one of the great writers of the western world, Ernest Hemingway. The first book that I saw was titled *For Whom the Bell Tolls*. I didn't pay attention to its thickness or how heavy it was - I just simply grabbed it and ran. Well, I didn't realize that I had my work cut out for me – never mind that it was

112

thick, heavy, long, and in many places unable to hold all of my attention. At the outset the book invokes its namesake, a poem by John Donne:

> "No man is an *Iland*, intire of it selfe; every man is a peece of the *Continent*, a part of the *maine*; if a *Clod* bee washed away by the *Sea*, *Europe* is the lesse, as well as if a *Promontorie* were, as well as if a *Mannor* of thy *friends* or of *thine owne* were; any man's *death* diminishes *me*, because I am involved in *Mankinde*; And therefore never send to know for whom the *bell* tolls; It tolls for *thee*."

I decided to title my book review "For Whom Did the Bell Toll?" It was several weeks later where we dutifully reported to our section, which usually numbered roughly 15 Cadets, and I knew going in that one of us was going to be selected to make a presentation on their book review. What caught my eye was that when we got in the room I noticed that the head of the Department of English and various other professors were in the back, when all of a sudden it occurred to me there was something going on here. My guess was that somebody or several people kind of took a look at my book review and figured, "Okay, here's another smart aleck Cadet trying to pull one over on the English department."

Well, I wasn't wrong. It was not long after we were seated when the instructor, our professor said, "Cadet Arnhym, we'd like you to make a presentation on your book review." I really didn't have a great deal of time to think about it, but I gave it as much thought as I could as I traversed the few steps from my seat to the front of the classroom. I then looked to the back at a rather ominous group of officers and professors waiting for what I was going to say.

To the best of my recollection, this is what I said:

"Over the course of this particular term, we've been reading a number of books and the works of many great writers and in every instance the professor would look at us and say, 'What did Keats – or Shakespeare or Kipling or Churchill – mean when they said...?' And one of the Cadets would report with what he thought was intended by a particular passage or a particular chapter."

"At the end of that, there were at least 15 opinions on the table, and to nobody's shock, when we were all finished, the professor would come up with the English department's understanding of that particular phrase, paragraph, or chapter. I inferred from that that it was perfectly okay to have an opinion and it would not necessarily coincide with that of the Department of English."

"Based on such an open dialogue and the opportunity for each of us to think independently, as I read this book by a very distinguished author, and I reflected on the book's invocation, 'For whom did the toll, the bell tolled for thee,' I failed to hear a thing. I did not hear anything. I didn't get the message. There was nothing profound that captured my attention. In my judgment, that should be considered okay because 'thee' didn't say everybody. What it really says is that each one of us should be entitled to his or her opinion and that should be okay."

As it turned out, they happily agreed with me, and I maxed the oral presentation as well as the book review. But going forward, it actually taught me something – to face a situation, to be ready to make a quick decision, and then move on with it. It taught me to get to the point just as quickly as I could.

Take Control

I'm not going to ask you to read through the many chapters and pages that are in this book without trying to guess or figure out where am I going or what this is all about. What I am telling you is that at the end of every day you need to take control of the situation, disregard voicemail, disregard email, disregard everything extraneous going on, and even – if you have to – shut the door.

Then you go back to your checklist, to your notes, wherever they are, look at those priority items and then tick them off one by one. Clearly you're not going to get the whole list done, but at least have a couple that you have already predetermined in your mind, "These are the things that I have to get done today, irrespective of every other obstacle and of everything else that's going on."

In a previous chapter, I mentioned *Good to Great*, in which the main idea is to get the right person on the bus. My question is how many pages and how many chapters did I have to go through before I figured that out? Incidentally, just about everybody ultimately figures it out.

In this book, I make frequent reference to the universal practice of starting everything and finishing nothing. The way to avoid that trap is to take control of your actions and take control of your day to make certain that those things that you started, you completed. It may only be two or three, but at least pick out a couple of priority things that you know that you cannot afford to push over until tomorrow.

The 1st Hussars of the armored primary reserve regiment of the Canadian forces use the Latin motto *"Hodie non cras."* It translates as, "Today not tomorrow." I love that motto. If you want to adopt that as your own, I doubt the 1st Hussars would object.

I graduated from West Point in 1953. By all means go ahead and do the math, then you'll get a good idea of how many careers I've had and how old I am. I have learned more lessons than I can easily count. Quite candidly, I would happily put a bumper sticker on my car that says, "I'm done learning," but we can't afford to do that. You want the people who work for you to be cutting-edge. You want somebody that has the best available information at their fingertips so that they can get their job done, so that you can get the best possible result - those you work for expect the same.

I'm Not Done Learning

I find that on a daily basis I continue to learn, and I think that's a good thing. Through the chapters of this book, the underlying message is that there are a number of things that you can be doing to make certain that it's not about starting everything and finishing nothing.

We all have to learn how to deal with change – we have to surround ourselves with good people that we can trust, we need to be decisive and decide to decide, we cannot assume that it cannot be done, nor is it easier if you do it yourself. More often than not, as you will reach a fork in the road or an obstacle that will keep you from following your plan, you will have to start over. You will always have to deal or work with others to get things done, so you must be accountable and hold others accountable. If there is a single skill you must practice constantly, it is listening. Listening doesn't just help you gather information about the world around you – it helps to make sure you're heard by others, for people are more receptive to those who listen than they are to those who don't.

One of the jobs that I held on one of my two tours in Vietnam was Commander of a Task Force that was defending Cam Ranh Bay. One of the biggest threats we faced were the Viet Cong sappers – underwater swimmers, who would enter the bay carrying explosive devices and attach them to ships that were anchored there delivering munitions, food, and supplies for our forces in South Vietnam. Their detection was not an easy task, as they came in at night and it was dark. This wasn't dark like a suburban street at night - this was dark like moonless nights in the wilderness. We did have side-looking radar on patrol boats that could detect motion, though I didn't think this was very effective, and furthermore, I regarded it as passive. Because of this, I would instruct my people to fill their patrol boats up with hand grenades, which they would then indiscriminately throw into the water. I based this approach on another lesson I had learned in commanding a battalion operating from firebases. It was called "H and I" – harassing and interdicting – firing randomly into the jungle as a deterrent for either the Viet Cong or North Vietnamese to approach our position. Because it was indiscriminate, and could happen at any time at any location, it was effective at keeping intruders away and kept us safe at night.

Tossing hand grenades indiscriminately into Cam Ranh Bay wasn't anything you'd find in the field manual, but I think it protected a lot of lives. It also taught me a lot about adapting techniques from one setting to another. By the way, it worked.

I told you before that my journey started at age nine. My parents decided that we should take a trip up to West Point, which at the time was about 60 miles north of where we were living in New Jersey. My parents thought from an educational perspective, visiting West Point would be not only a unique opportunity to see a little bit of history, but would open up my eyes to some of the things that made our nation what it is today. When we got there we did the kind of things that just about every tourist and visitor thinks when they get up to a place like West Point – we took a tour and we saw as much of West Point and the historical buildings in a couple of hours that we could. During this time I was impressed with the grandeur and the splendor of this magnificent place on the Hudson River. West Point sits strategically at a point in the Hudson River where many years ago a chain was stretched across the Hudson River to Constitution Island to stop the British Navy from reaching their troops in New York.

The buildings, the view, and looking up the Hudson, were all awe-inspiring moments. The Cadet Chapel sits majestically on the side of a hill mass above West Point. Everything about the place spoke to a nine-year-old boy. As I tried to take all of this in, I saw the cadets, each one of which impressed me beyond words. I decided then and there that I was going to go to West Point, I wanted to be a Cadet, I wanted that four-year experience at this magnificent place, and I wanted to serve in the Army as an Officer with a career in the United States Army.

The Practice of Discipline

Over the next ten years that determination never left me. Everything I did, every item on my checklist, was a step toward that goal. Every day I thought about it, every week I did something about it, every month I'd check in with myself and hold myself accountable, asking myself the question – am I going to achieve that goal? Finally, on the first of July 1949, I entered the United States Military Academy and graduated four years later as a Second Lieutenant.

What I started, I finished. Although when I finished, I realized it wasn't the end but another beginning. I understood then that my professional life would be an unending succession of finish lines. Since graduation there have been new goals and new finish lines, and while it could be argued that it's not my persona to start everything and finish nothing, at least I finished as much as I could. I tried to make certain that the things I finished were the important ones.

Every one of us starts the day with the best of intentions – we have all these tasks outlined, we've identified those items which should receive the highest possible priority, and yet, by the time we reach the end of the day, we find that we have literally started everything and finished nothing. The bottom line is that if you had a plan, you didn't stick to it. If you had priorities, the chances are that you were deflected from those priorities because something more important interfered.

The simple truth is, that starting everything and finishing nothing cannot be solved by not just simply sticking to the plan, but by asking yourself at the end day, "What is it that I came in here to do?" "What was my plan of action?" Stop everything you may be doing, look back at how you entered the day in the first place, and start over and select the highest-priority items that have not been accomplished.

It's really about discipline. It's really about selecting a time of the day where you stop what you're doing and go back to where you came in the door in the first place with the best of intentions. I do this every day at approximately four o'clock – I stop listening to voicemail, I stop looking at my email, I shut down all the things on my desk that have gotten my attention during the course of the day and I go back to that top-line item on my task list and say to myself, "Rolfe, you just simply have got to get that done."

In conclusion, it's really up to you.

Chapter 8

Networking and Relationship Building

If you want to avoid the starting-everything-and-finishing-nothing, you should delete the word "networking" from your vocabulary. Nobody ever finishes networking. I learned this the hard way. When I arrived in Tampa, I went on a "networking rampage" to find potential new opportunities for myself and to let people know what I can do. That little engine inside of me saw more tracks! However, to my dismay, they learned who I was, but not what I did or what I was looking to do. Networking events can be lunches (typically with a speaker), dinner, trade shows, conventions, even parties. More often than not, you exchange business cards with someone and then go on to the next suspect, furiously gathering a stack of pasteboard to replace the stack you've given away.

You get back to your office, where you have calls, messages, projects, and meetings waiting. You then dump the business cards while you get some work done. Days later, guilt steps in, and you try to find out what you started and did not finish. There are often multiple piles of cards, and you can't remember where or when you met the individual whose card you're now staring at blankly.

Worst of all, you can't even remember what they're all about.

There are five rules for avoiding this trap.

Rule number one: don't exchange cards. Present your card, not unlike what you see happen in the Asian culture. When you present the card, they look at it and form a mental picture of your card, as you can of them looking at your card. Then, take the card they have presented to you and make a note on the back about something personal or professional that differentiates that individual. Plan a meeting at a Ritz Carlton and note that the staff members "present their business cards."

Rule number two: At an event, maintain eye contact with the person you just met and to whom you present the card. Don't look past them to someone that may appear to be, in your view, more important than the person that you're talking to. Be well assured that people know the that-person-may-be-more-important look. The way to avoid being known as the one who looks past others for the more important people, simply remind yourself that the person you are talking to is the most important person in your world at that moment.

Rule number three: Don't cling to the person. Move on. Time after time I have noticed that people head to someone they know and then they hang on to them like a *Titanic* survivor. I have walked up to complete strangers who are then blown away because I approached them, making them feel important. I always make a point of introducing myself to the speaker. They love it. I've also approached celebrities, politicians, and other personages with similar results. I've introduced myself to the

Secretary of Defense, President Ford, Bob Hope, George Steinbrenner, and a long list of others you would know.

In the case of George Steinbrenner, he was so pleased that I introduced myself while others were hanging back that we entered into an extraordinarily interesting conversation. I commended him and the New York Yankees for consistently hosting the Color Guard from West Point at their opening day events. This led into a question from him: "So, how can I help you?" I didn't stand on ceremony; at the time I was working with *Forbes Magazine* with a view towards getting an article on West Point in an upcoming edition. I told him that if the article was to appear in *Forbes Magazine* they were not necessarily going to do this as a freebie and I needed a sponsor to make that happen. Without even blinking he said, "How much?" What resulted is the New York Yankees sponsored a section in an upcoming issue of *Forbes Magazine* on West Point.

Rule number four: Introduce yourself to each person at the table where you are seated, and to as many people as you can reach.

Rule number five: Follow up. "Networking" is introductions. After the introductions, you need to shift into the "building the relationship" mode. I would submit that this is a lost art. I remember a banker in Beverly Hills. His bank charged him with establishing himself within the community by working himself up through the Chamber of Commerce and other organizations to a position of leadership. Needless to say, it was the bank's intent that all the while everyone in the Chamber and/or other organizations would know which bank he worked for, with the clear intent of developing a business relationship.

Well, this individual was excellent at reaching out. He was superb in his ability to work himself up through the chairs and ultimately was the President of multiple organizations within the Beverly Hills community. However, there was one rub: everybody knew him by name but very few knew the company or the bank he worked for.

At the same time, there was a second person with a similar mandate from his employer. He was quieter in his approach, but equally effective. In his particular case, he would always reach out and call attention to his company and his name followed. You have to be very careful in building your relationships that you don't forget where you came from (i.e., the company you work for). At the end of the day, your mission is to extend your company's outreach into the community and build relationships for the mutual advantage of your company and those of your new contacts.

Beyond Networking

One example that I recall in particular was the Senior Vice President for Marketing for Delta Airlines in the Pasadena area. This guy was amazing. He was clearly a "people person" and, as the CEO of the Pasadena Chamber of Commerce, I facilitated a path for him. He ultimately became our Vice President for Membership. When he started out, his various committees on retention and new member recruitment were poorly attended. At each meeting he decided that he would distribute some item from Delta Airlines. It could be a pen. It could be a bag. It could be almost anything. He also made the meetings fun but it was always very, very clear that he was representing Delta Airlines.

Because of his personal energy, and perhaps the toys that he brought with him, the attendance grew to unprecedented levels. Instead of a few people sitting around a table, the room was always full. We used to say that none of us would think of going any place unless Delta Airlines went there. Well, that's a little bit extreme. I think you get the point. Networking without relationship building is starting without finishing.

Because I have never let myself lose sight of this, people have come to realize how useful I am to them. One, I'm constantly out there meeting new people and as a result have a very deep database. Through that database alone, I have been branded as a "go-to." Anyone in sales, or anyone who is a CEO, should build relationships conscientiously and strive to be the "go-to." But this is not just about being known — it is about who and what you can do. It means that you must also stay informed and be interesting; it is not enough that you read the sports page. Although it is a simple given, it is an effective one.

Everyone in your professional community should know you as the go-to. Let me make a small diversion here to mention how important it is to define yourself - it is critical for others to know who you are and what you do. When I was the CEO of the Long Beach Chamber of Commerce, it, like every other chamber of commerce, would host a networking breakfast. The intent obviously was to generate business. At these breakfasts, people would get up, mumble their names, and then sit down. Then the next person would repeat the process. Meanwhile, people would continue to eat their breakfasts, drink their coffee, look at their notes, or talk to their neighbors - very little attention was being paid to the person making the self-introduction.

Based on that experience, I decided that we needed to ramp this up a tad, and I started to push the notion of people standing up but not only giving their name but to call out to the attendees their tagline. Curiously, not everyone had a tagline. This of course forced them to think about it, and the result was unbelievable. One lady who was the owner and general manager for a mortuary came up with the following tagline. It is better to know us and not need us than need us and not know us. I thought that was absolutely dynamite.

As a matter of fact, think about whether tagline could apply to you and your business. As long as you're not in Long Beach (where it's already being used by one of the mortuaries), it could help define both your mission and your role in your community. As part of relationship building, I have also learned the importance of having a target list. Obviously it should include people that you should know and businesses that you want to do business with. Work your relationship building skills on these people to make sure you're moving in the direction you want to go. Let me be very clear here: it matters not if you are in sales or a CEO – maintain a "must list" of companies or individuals that you need to meet and do business with.

Committed to Commitments
Develop habits that define you for the people you deal with. Everyone who deals with me, for example, recognizes that I am committed to my commitments. I reach out once a week, typically on a Wednesday, to

reaffirm my commitments for the following week. And then I show up no matter what.

Here's another rule for living well. If someone asks you to have breakfast or lunch or to meet with him or her on a date where you already have a commitment, don't simply say, "I'm sorry but I'm busy that day." Reply with multiple scheduling opportunities - it saves a lot of time. In fact, it's a good idea to not only agree on a date and time but follow up as well. As I said before, my pet peeve is the missing of scheduled dates by those that do not share my same sense of commitment.

This leads me to conclude that something or someone else is more important that I am. This is not exactly the way to build a good relationship with me. I've often thought I would like to have a second bumper sticker that says, "If you make a commitment, stick to it." Sometimes I feel like I'm the only one out here honoring my commitments. Maybe it's a generational issue, or maybe business etiquette has changed. Let me suggest, however, that if you always honor your commitments, you will differentiate yourself from the herd, which is half the battle of selling yourself.

I will typically have my breakfast or lunch meetings in one of two clubs where I am a member. I always sit in the same place by strategic intent. By sitting in a highly visible location and at the same table, I see everyone who comes in the door, and everyone who comes in sees me. I love it when someone stops by and says, "I always see you here. What do you do?" That's the foundation for another relationship. Furthermore, my guests at these meetings are amazed at the number of people that come by and say hello and reintroduce themselves. This gives me the opportunity to introduce them to my guest. I can't count the number of times one of my guests has said, "You must know everybody." Well, isn't that the goal?

Don't restrict your relationship building to the people on your target list - build relationships with their gatekeepers, too. Over the years, I have learned to get to know them by name and to know a little bit about each one of them. I make it a point to engage them upon my arrival. It has proven to be a win-win relationship. By virtue of that relationship, I always get in the door, and I always get priority when it comes to getting on somebody's calendar. But here's the most important part. I make a gatekeeper feel important, and they share that with their boss, which strengthens my relationship with the boss.

Find the Real Person
As I noted before, it is possible to find the real person behind the veil of a businessperson in their office. By commenting on one of their personal items, I make the conversation about them. When I am asked a question about myself during that discussion, I work hard at turning it around so that I can deploy my listening skills at every opportunity.

Too many of us are so pleased to get in somebody's office that we hit the "press to talk" button and don't stop because we're in a hurry to make our point. This is totally wrong. By listening, I can find out exactly what I need to know. More often than not, as a result of the conversation, common interests are identified, and you begin to build that relationship. It doesn't make any difference if you're in an office environment or at an event. Being a good listener is the key to building a relationship.

128

Some studies have suggested that it takes seven touches before a client relationship has been established. I would dispute that number and can generally take it down to two or three, which I do by listening.

When looking for new members for Vistage, a by-invitation organization, I work to establish trust, common interests, mutual respect, and rapport. I find out what is important to them and, at the same time, what my other group members would gain by virtue of their being part of Vistage, as well as what my members can give to them if they come on board. The Vistage model brings CEOs and senior executives together in a think-tank type environment. No two-group members are from the same business classification. When I'm looking for new members for the group, I find out very quickly what their hot buttons are. What keeps them awake at night? Where is their pain? What is it that they're trying to decide or they can't decide?

By asking questions and by getting them to talk about themselves, how they got there, and what they're dealing with, I always keep the conversation about them. I hold off on who I am or what I have done until they ask. However, by the time that they ask that, they have usually exhausted themselves recounting their own story. I am totally fine with that. There's no difference with that approach in your business relationships. In looking to identify top CEOs for Vistage whom I can help to grow professionally and help them grow their companies, I am building the same kind of client relationships as you are no matter what your business is.

My relationship-building motto is "no one is safe." Wherever I am or go I make a point of meeting someone new. By virtue of my work, as I noted earlier, I keep a full schedule. What that really says is that relationship building should be inherent in everything you do during the course of a business day. Learn to appreciate people and to be fascinated by their unique stories. There is a corollary to that, and that is that people you meet should be able to look past how you describe yourself or whatever is written on your business card. To be a go-to person with a big database is okay, but you do not want to be a talking head with nothing behind it. Make it a point to be well read and informed.

Be Someone They Want to Know

I make sure I get past the sports pages. I watch the news. I read a professional book each month. I work very hard to be interesting and someone others want to talk to or with. I don't want to be identified as sales-y or someone totally focused on the sale. I want to be identified as someone that others want to connect with, that others want to learn from, that others want to just simply talk to. It could be argued that all of this eats the clock. Of course it does, but the ROI is enormous.

It goes without saying that if you're going to build relationships, face-to-face contact trumps email, text messages, and voicemail. Face-to-face contact is the warm version of the cold call.

By the way, when you look at your allocation of time on a daily or a weekly basis, sitting behind your desk will only result in a close working relationship with your desk. You want to grow your business, not the part of you that you sit on. Most of these principles apply at home, too. On the goals matrix for every one of my CEOs and Senior Executives, I have a column that speaks to personal goals.

What I find more often than not is someone who says that their goal is to create a better balance between work and life. The horrible reality is that this is a great goal, but so few of us can accomplish it. Each generation has a different view of work-life balance, and every CEO is constantly challenged by it.

Relationships at Home

Well, some weekends I find myself in a work-play-work scenario. My goal always is to get to play-work-play. I find that if I'm going to accomplish the latter, then I need to draw some lines in the sand, and one of those is that on Saturdays and Sundays at precisely 6:00 p.m., I stop whatever I'm doing and my wife and I meet in the family room for a one-on-one (a term that I learned in Vistage). This is where we communicate and just go over stuff. Sometimes we may just sit there and watch the news. In other instances it becomes that opportunity for the longer stories, which obviously replace the quick bullet items that you get when you walk in the door.

In one of those one-on-one sessions with my wife, I asked her to come up with a list of 10 things that she wanted to see or do with no time limit attached. What was funny is that for a while she sat there and nothing appeared on the paper, then all of a sudden her hand went flying across the pages and I had to caution her just 10. I made a similar list, but my main purpose was to find out those things that were important to her that maybe I hadn't picked up on. To my complete surprise, her list didn't look anything like mine. I would submit that sometimes we fail to apply the principles that we work so hard to put in place in the work place. We don't see their application at home.

For me, these weekend one-on-ones are precious and protected time. In all my relationship building, I try not to lose sight of the most important relationship: that with your spouse. Presumably, that doesn't need building so much as it needs maintenance. Make the time for it, as it will ultimately mean more to you than any business deals.

There's a sort of tired joke with which people often tease each other. You meet someone and say, "It's nice to see you." They reply, "It's nice to be seen." It's not much of a joke, but it speaks to a deep human desire. People like to be seen, but even more than that, they like to be known. When it comes to taglines, "It's nice to be known" would do nicely for just about any of us - isn't that the purpose of relationship building?

Finally, this is one place that shouldn't worry about starting everything and finishing nothing, because you will never finish relationship building. It is the work of a lifetime.

As I write this book, some 30 years after the move of the Army-Navy game to Pasadena, the unexpected happened in the span of two weeks. We were traveling in the British Isles and taking an excursion off the ship when I spotted a member of our group who was wearing a West Point jacket. I asked him if he was a graduate, to which he replied that he was not, but his daughter was. As it turns out, she was one of two Cadets who were my link to the Corps of Cadets for liaison purposes. How does this happen? A week later I found myself at West Point for a football game where I met the new Commandant of Cadets. I told him about this book, and it took my breath away when he told me that he was on the football team that played in the Rose Bowl that year. Not only that, but he was the player that threw the first tackle and reserved the ball being carried off to his teammate Napoleon McCallum, who unfortunately ran for a touchdown in the first minute of the game. My relationships are so deep that I have yet to travel anywhere without running into someone that I know or at least by one degree of separation.

Chapter 9

Managing Your Time

"Are you busy?"

How many times a day are you asked that question? Of course you're busy, but the person asking that question isn't really asking if you're busy. He or she is asking for your approval or for additional guidance – translation: another interrupter. More often than not, you will take the time. The chances are very good that this conversation will upset your schedule and perhaps even push you into the "finishing nothing" territory. But one of the things about being a leader is being accessible: to your followers, to your colleagues, even to your enemies. Busy people just figure it out, even if it means a visible checklist. Candidly, I keep a 3 by 5 index card in my shirt pocket. Remember the guy who had over 250 tasks buried in his iPhone?

As the CEO of the Beverly Hills Chamber of Commerce I enjoyed a very close working relationship with the Mayor, who as it turns out was a former President of the Beverly Hills Chamber of Commerce. Therefore he knew what to expect from the Chamber of Commerce, and from me in particular. One of the things he could expect was access: that I was there, and he did not have to go through some gatekeeper or voice mail menu to find me. When he wanted me, he wanted me. I finally decided to install a separate phone line that went straight to the Mayor's office. I put a red phone on my desk to connect to that line. After that, any time the Mayor wanted, my red phone rang.

Of course, anyone who saw that red phone on my desk wanted to have a connection to it. It was good discipline for me, and good practice for my firefighting skills to keep those connections from happening. But I had a particular relationship with the Mayor and succeeding mayors, and that relationship was embodied in that red phone, so I held firm in protecting it. It was about communications and being able to respond quickly. I understood his time was valuable, and he understood mine was as well. You can't connect everybody to your red phone, but in this case the Mayor was my red phone person. That simple act had a major side effect: a close-working relationship with city leaders.

I am not suggesting that you put a red phone on your desk. What I am saying is that there may be decision makers who should enjoy direct and immediate communication. Yes, that can be interruptive, and yes, that can drive you off course, and yes, it may mean that an entire day is shot, and you can't get to those things that you felt that you needed to get done. But you may (and probably do) have a professional relationship that requires immediate and focused attention. Give it your attention when it's required, because that's what busy people do.

"I Know You're In There"
How can you get your work done in a world in which people have claims on your time? One of the simplest

techniques is to establish some quiet time before your business goes live. In Beverly Hills, we had offices with windows that faced the street. I would always get in early, I'd pull the shades, and I'd try to hide out in there to get some work done before people started showing up. I can't tell you how many times somebody would go by and would knock on the window and say, "Rolfe, I know you're in there." I followed that same regimen in every CEO position that I held. Fortunately, the others did not have street-level windows.

At 4:00 p.m., I stop what I'm doing and shut off any interruptions and go back to my to-do list and to my desk calendar and ask myself the question: "What is it that I planned to do today that I have not done, and what are those priority tasks that absolutely have got to get done today?"

No matter what else I plan on doing during a day, I schedule a given amount of time for business development. Whether that's calling a new client or calling an existing client and looking for a referral, or whether it's a follow-up, business development time gets priority attention, and my day does not end unless I've devoted at least a half an hour to the sales side of the house. On some days, I've met with my sales manager at the end of the day, or I've undertaken those priority contacts that I know are absolute imperatives. We all know there are things we will not finish by the end of the day, but there are some things that simply cannot slide off until tomorrow.

Part of managing time is knowing what your people are doing. Are they managing and using the time as you would have them do? Therefore, walking the four corners, whether you do that at the beginning of the day, at the end of the day, or both. This is not as important as the very step itself because this is a quick way to find out if those tasks are being accomplished that you expect to be accomplished. Needless to say, you're not going to do it all and you're not going to do it yourself. We have already covered that. It's your people who are going to do it. There is an Army axiom, "what gets inspected, gets done." The facts are that your employees take pride in telling you that the job has been done. On time and correctly is another issue.

The Weekly To-Do Report

I briefly mentioned one of the tools that I've always used to ensure that my people are spending their time well is that by 4 p.m. every Friday, I require a to-do report. It has three sections in it. The first section are those top five priorities for next week, the second is what they got done and what they did not get done, and third is any questions that they have of me or if they need to meet with me or something is not clear and they need additional guidance. I have found that if the priorities are out of sync with my expectations, I can adjust them before Monday gets started. If I find a task was not done then I have the opportunity very quickly to find out what it is that got in the path. Maybe some event or activity has gotten in the way, and I need to address it. Sometimes I have even found that I am the blockage because I didn't provide enough guidance or instruction. The to-do report is a simple one-page document. It's a good tool for holding people accountable, but it's also an important tool in managing my own time and the time of others. While you may get push back initially, it is amazing how quickly this tool was embraced and how much time it saved.

Here's another tool: any time that I have a meeting it goes for exactly 59 minutes. Everybody who knows me knows that. If I call a meeting for 8:00 a.m., they know that it will be completed at 8:59, and if somebody is still talking we're all going to walk out. If I'm conducting a meeting with a board or some other group over which I don't have as much direct control, I have a timeline for that meeting that I share with the Chair or with some other person to make sure that we stay on track. If somebody throws something into the oscillator unexpectedly, we throw it over on a parking lot and if time permits, we get back to it.

For lunch meetings with a lot of people, a speaker, and so forth, I put the word out that the meeting is going to go from 12:00 until 1:29. This way, people do not start leaking out the door at about 1:15 or 1:20. If they know precisely when the meeting will end, they will stay. Before I did that, I found people would start leaving because they didn't know when it was going to be over, and we had to expect a certain number of people to start leaving after lunch. That stopped dead cold the moment that I advertised a 1:29 finish time. I held to it slavishly, even if I had to go up and jerk the speaker by the belt and pull away the microphone – in jest – but it had the desired effect. You know what happened? People stayed past 1:29 all the way up to 1:45 or later. It's amazing what a simple step like that will do so that you can better manage your time and be more respectful of the time of others.

Predictability is an important component in time management and certainly on the part of your people. They know that by a certain time you're going to make a decision. You're not going to shove it off for tomorrow because you got too busy. My definition of the leader is the decider, however, the true leader will let you know when that decision should be made.

"I Was Busy"

Here's what used to drive me crazy. At a staff meeting, I'd go around the table and I'd ask this question, "Okay, what is it you're telling your spouse or your significant other when you get home at night?"

More often than not, their answer would be, "Well, I was busy."

And I would ask, "Okay, busy doing what?"

My staff got that message that at the end of the day, if you can't point to something you did other than respond to calls and go to meetings and handle interruptions and what not, you just lost a day. They already knew that they could ill afford to make that statement. Undone tasks have a nasty way of piling up. Were all too familiar with the term "busy week." We need a new term: "finish work."

Going back to my time at the Electro-Optical Systems Division of Xerox in Pasadena as Co-Program manager for the MILES program, one of my responsibilities was for the reporting. The reporting component of this contract carried a bill of slightly in excess of a million dollars all by itself. We were expected to provide the government with a report on a quarterly basis and it included a description of the stage of the design at that moment. It was always hard to get that report pulled together. Engineers, being what they are and how they think and function, will continue working on something until you stop them. They're going to keep going as long as they can to design that perfect widget or whatever it is. So it was a major task to get the report off in time. Never mind they can't write or speak, as this became my job in presentations for our government clients.

I would always include in the report a statement to the government, which in essence said, "As of this date, this is the current design for the various components of our project. Unless we hear to the contrary within thirty days, we will proceed with the next phase." Of course, nobody paid attention. But that wasn't our problem. We kept on going. Later in the course of the project, however, they would come back to us and say, "Wait a minute, we want to make this particular change."

We just told them, "We give you the opportunity to make those changes, to disapprove or to take whatever action you deemed appropriate and you did not do that, you did not exercise it. This program is going to stay on time, and it's going to stay on budget, if you want us to do something else then we will be happy to incorporate that in a side contract in a different time line and a different funding." You know what, that's exactly what they did. At the end of that program we delivered on schedule and on budget, *and* we had an additional contract to run out some of those great ideas that later were integrated downstream as the project developed. The bottom line was that there was no time or money wasted. I have to add that they live and die by the acronym and thirst for new words. As we were preparing for one of our briefings, we spoke about the point that they were always trying to invent new engineer speak. I suggested that, since they were so thirsty for new language, that maybe we should invent a word for them, and in my opening remarks I will thrust that word in a few times and we will see how quickly after they respond that they will begin to use that word – my guess is that I'll give it two minutes. We would put the bet on after we would get to the end our presentation, and I would open up my comments by saying that we've identified a number of pacing items that could influence this project. Translation: interrupters. Within two minutes they were using the term pacing item.

From Combat to the Civilian Sector
In combat you don't want to be predictable and the same is true in business. That's the whole idea. One of my jokes with sales people is that I will often tell them if somebody doesn't call you, pick up the phone and call somebody. Cold calls are a good thing. As a matter of fact, I would tell them I used cold calls all the time in Vietnam, and it worked very well.

I know I refer back to my combat experience a lot, so you are entitled to ask how combat is different from the civilian sector. It's pretty simple. In combat, I knew who was shooting at me. In the business sector, you just don't know. It could be a competitor, or it could be somebody that wants to enter the same market as you with a similar product at a lower cost, or any number of things. I would submit that in today's super-charged, highly competitive economy, it's a lot like combat without the noise. I have to believe as well that as veterans of the wars in Iraq and Afghanistan enter the workforce, they will quickly get the analogy and in all likelihood before our future leaders. What I learned from over 20 years in the Army, and from combat in particular, was the need for discipline. The consequences if a task was not done and on time directly impacted mission accomplishment. Task or job not done can cost countless dollars and impact profits

How often have you been frustrated by subordinates who don't get the job done when it has to get done? You're left trying to explain to someone else why that is, the costs begin to mount and, in the long run, you lose business. At some level, managing time is up to you, and you should live your professional life the way you think you should. But time management is crucial if you're going to get the things done that you said you're going to get done - pushing something from Monday to Tuesday, to Wednesday to Thursday to Friday, just does not work because it comes down to time and dollars.

Missing deadlines means dramatic cost increases, many of us have failed to plan incremental goals to begin with. You have to ask yourself what caused the missed deadline and who or what were the interrupters. Was it the lack of information? Were your efforts were diverted, or were you overwhelmed? The moment we start moving those deadlines out, it becomes a prescription for disaster.

As I've listened to the various CEOs and senior executives that I've worked with, I've come to understand we live in a time in which our people are not always necessarily present in the building, never mind fully present in mind and body. Like I said before, look at your children texting under the table while you're having dinner. Go to a meeting and see how many people are on electronic devices while the presentation is in progress or while somebody is talking. I would ask you the question – Are you here? And, if you can't be here, then where are you? Or, if you can't be here, then go there.

"Made Stupid by His Smartphone"
Managing time today is both an art and a science. All these mobile devices were supposed to make it easier to

manage time. They promised to allow us to be in two places at once, but they have never fulfilled that promise. You can't be two places at once, even if you have the latest smartphone. All the smartphone does is multiply the number of choices you have and it often gives you so many choices that you can't pick one. That, paradoxically, makes you seem stupid. That could be an epitaph: "Made stupid by his smartphone." At some point, human intervention becomes necessary.

If you can't manage time and/or your tools, then don't expect to accomplish the tasks at the end of the day that you set out to complete. Finally, I need to take up something I have touched on before: work-life balance. The good news is, at the end of the day, you go home. The bad news is that you bring your smartphones and iPads with you. Each of us needs to establish our own work-life balance, our own formula that works for us. But you must have some time to think, and you must have some time to do those things that are important to your family and to your well-being. I set aside specific time every Saturday and every Sunday for golf and tennis, because it's important. I protect that time.

At the same time, you need to look at your weekend schedule, never mind your night schedule, and ask, "At what level is my business and my other activities intruding on my personal life and my well-being?" You do that and manage boundaries.

If somebody asks me to go to a meeting or to go someplace on Saturday, they can forget it. Because I'm going to be on the tennis court at 8:00 a.m., and I'll be on the golf course at 11:30. On Sunday, it's church and then golf.

Everybody should have protected times. Your work life does not have to be 24/7. You can manage to have a life.

As I mentioned in the last chapter, my wife and I have a one-on-one every Saturday and every Sunday at 6:00 p.m. That time is in concrete. I come out of my office or I stop what I'm doing at 6:00 p.m. because it is time for the two of us to share a drink, just to listen, or to do something together. Be well assured that if I'm not managing my time and not out there seated next to her at 6:00, I hear about it. I wouldn't have it any other way. You need to tell yourself to be more sensitive to others and to do a better job of managing your time, not only for your business, but also for the well-being in your own personal life and marital satisfaction.

Chapter 10

Now Firing?

As a CEO, I dreaded telling somebody that they were being fired or even that they were not performing up to my level of expectation. But when tasks are not done correctly or on time, sometimes you need to have that talk.

One of the most frequent pieces of advice given to managers is hire slow and fire fast. You need to operate that way if you're going to get the right people on the bus and in the right seats. In fact, getting the right people on the bus may not go far enough. It's my experience you also need to get them all facing in the same direction. Bus analogies notwithstanding, if things are not getting done, and you're not getting what you need to have done, you may not have the right people around you. If you don't have the right people, you may have to make some changes. At some level, CEOs live in fear. While cash flow tops the list, fear of firing is right up there because you dread the search and interview process, never mind the ramp-up time.

However, getting the right people on the bus is a goal and not a way of life. Things change. Your company may be growing rapidly. Its culture may be changing. You may

145

have employees who performed adequately before the change but who can't function well now. You may have employees who have ridden the growth wave to the next level and aren't suited to that level. A bookkeeper may not be ready to be a controller or a CFO. A growing sales team or expanding footprint may challenge a vice president of sales. Frankly, there are some people that just have moss growing on their north side, and totally lack motivation and initiative.

A long time ago, we recognized that you needed to adjust your management style to the differences between introverted and extroverted employees. We're way beyond that now. Today's workforces are multigenerational, and it seems each generation has their own value system. Each generation presents its own degree of difficulty, each one has different standards and value systems and each one requires – for lack of a better terminology – a different manager to employee relationship. Volumes have been written on this, and the hills are alive with the various instruments that you can use. One that almost pops into my head immediately is where you sort people as red, blue, yellow, and green. Each color has particular motivations and each requires a different style of interaction, but I find that learning the colors makes me forget I'm dealing with people rather than paint samples. There is a lesson here: be sure to call it like it is and don't invent new words to describe the obvious.

Think about your role as a parent. Too often we forget that our children expect us to be their parent and not their friend. At the same time, too often in the workplace, we forget that our employees are not our friends. At some point downstream there is hopefully room for friendship, and you cultivate that relationship through various events and activities. But never, ever forget that they are your employees, because you do them a disservice when you do.

What Is a Work Ethic?

When I got to Tampa, as I looked at many of the businesses and listened to various people in the workplace, the first thing that struck me was that to many, "work ethic" might have been the name of a California rock group. It had no deeper significance to them than that. As I looked deeper into organizations, I found that expectations of employees have not always been clearly defined and, all too often, the culture was not clear when they were hired. There was a lack of accountability and job descriptions were vague. In some situations, there was no organization chart. People would work as part of a team or a task force, and in any given week or month; somebody could be shifted to a different leader or boss.

In today's workplace, leaders work very hard to provide for flexible hours - you could have two members of the family working, or you may have a single parent that is charged with the responsibility of dropping their children off at school/picking them up at the end of the day. This defies the traditional notion of eight to five. Then you have people who work from home – some or all of the time – and this hinders your ability to see your people at work during the workday, even though the word loses its meaning when people are connected 24/7.

Leaders can be frustrated by these circumstances. But it's possible to get around some of these frustrations by managing the organization's culture.

At West Point, we were graded every day. This doesn't mean of course that we did not have periodic examinations. We had those just like everybody else, but daily grading was a great benefit to us. You could come to class in any given day, and you might not be as well prepared as you could have been. But with daily grading, your bad days were offset by your good days, and at the end of the week or even the month, your ups and down would even themselves out.

The problem in today's workforce and workplace is that a manager may find that when there is erratic behavior on the part of an employee, what West Point might have just meant a lower grade for the day becomes a firing situation. It comes down to a number of things that as a leader that you can, and should, put in place. I have mentioned a number of tools so far in this book, like the weekly to-do report, that can help you monitor performance and make course corrections, but I want to make sure that this chapter emphasizes the importance of training. There is no such thing as too much training any more than there is such a thing as too much communication.

Training and Communication Support Morale
The brutal fact is that we don't set aside time for training at every level and we don't communicate on a sufficiently frequent level either. Daily huddles, walking the four corners, and routines like that can help ensure that people are on task and that they know what they're doing, but you can also use these informal one-to-one encounters to make sure they understand why they're doing what they're actually doing. This matters for performance, morale, and handling the unexpected.

We think we can eliminate communication problems by having more meetings or that we can control people's performance by playing the blame game. We need to learn to recognize the situation in which an individual is just not able to perform at the level of expectation. Recognizing that situation is the first step to firing. It may sound brutal, but think how often your people told you after you fired someone, "They should have been gone long ago." Frankly, it should not be a surprise to the fired employee, either.

Why do we avoid firing? Is it because of compassion? Or worse, it's too hard to start a search and train a new hire. Maybe we just don't want to admit to making a bad hire? Clearly the best course of action to avoid firing is the advice I mentioned before: hire slow. But also be sure to remember the second part: fire fast.

In any case, the best way to avoid firing is a five-point approach:

- A deliberate hiring process.
- A vigorous on-boarding plan.
- A planned and continuous training program.
- An open door to the manager's office.
- Close and continuous communication.

You have read earlier that I am not a fan of the "ready, fire, aim" style of management and I certainly abhor an organizational climate of fear. I do advocate a performance-based culture, with expectations clearly defined. I especially despise the organizational culture in which a manager earns his or her chops by firing someone. (It reminds of the street gangs that require members to kill someone for their initiation.) You might as well use my idea from earlier and put a sign outside that reads "Now Firing," which is the fast track to demoralization and stunted performance. A culture that is built on teamwork and team building should be the starting point. You want to foster a culture in which an employee says, "I want to go to work" rather than "I have to go to work."

The Mandate of Leadership

At the end of each day the CEO has to set the tone and be seen as a leader and the decider. It is the CEO who inspires loyalty. Too often CEOs forget how much they can damage the organization by not being seen as decisive. On any given day, you may have on your to-do list "Fire the Sales VP." And at the end of the day, you didn't do it. Why not? What got in the way? "He has been with us since the beginning," or "She is near retirement," or worse, "We have a personal relationship," or even worse yet, "He or she is a family member." These are not reasons for putting it off - they are different ways of saying you're not doing your job.

You may not have shared your to-do list with anyone (and I hope you don't, when it includes firing an employee), but when you don't act decisively the people who work for you can sense it. They know when you're hiding something from them; they know when you're hiding something from yourself. Human beings are the product of millions of years of social evolution, and our ability to read each other is highly refined, even if that ability is largely unconscious.

Try to think of yourself as a role model. Who was your role model? For my part, and driven by multiple careers, I had several. Employees appreciate the drive and dedication of someone whose desired epitaph is "Mentor," especially when his or her professional life does not seem to indicate this choice. They get inspiration every time that they meet with you and they see your energy and your desire to nurture and support those who work for you and your commitment to encourage them to perform, to grow, and to reach the next level of self-realization.

Above all, don't get angry with an under-performing employee. By the way, when I was angry, I was always a dead giveaway: my face turned red and I couldn't stop it. Before you lose your temper, ask yourself several questions:

- "Did I give them sufficient guidance and instruction?"
- "Did I constantly communicate with them and did they hear what I said?"
- "Did I open up opportunities to train them and to prepare them for the requirements that I had set for them?"

If you're still angry, find ways to deflect it. I am an avid tennis player on the weekend, and when I am carrying a ton of frustration, or sometimes anger with one or more employees, I tend to inscribe their name mentally on a tennis ball. During the course of the first game of the first set of the weekend, I hit that tennis ball just as hard as I can hit it. It was amazing how transferring that mental energy to a physical realm had a calming effect on me. Never mind that it forces me to pay attention to the number one requirement of any sport, and that is to keep your eye on the ball. Often someone will ask me, "Did you get rid of that anger in the first game, or was my name on that ball for an entire set?" Be well assured I never answer that question.

My point is that too frequently we make snap judgments about our people without realizing that we may be at fault. The fact that something didn't get done on any given day may be because we failed to communicate, give them that added piece of encouragement or instruction, or provided them with the motivation.

I hope I've made it clear that I don't subscribe to the "Now Firing" philosophy, but my people have got to know that a lack of performance, an inability to meet the standard, an inability to be a team player, or a failure to buy into organization's culture is going to get them helped out of the organization. When it's over, I have nearly always found my employees saying, "Why didn't you do that long ago?"

When you are starting everything and finishing nothing, look to see if you are somehow getting in your own way. If you can honestly satisfy yourself that you're not, look to see if there isn't one individual who's not on the team, who's not performing, or who's not acting as a participant in the organizational culture.

Then run out to your car and post a bumper sticker that says, "I'm tired of learning." Really?

Chapter 11

Dealing with Change

My first military assignment as a freshly minted second lieutenant was unusual for an "entry level" position. I was to report to the Infantry School at Fort Benning, Georgia. There I was going to learn all that I needed to know about being an Infantry Officer and how to lead and command soldiers in small units: first, a platoon of 41 men, and later an infantry company of a little over 150 men - pretty daunting for a brand new Second Lieutenant, 23 years old. Good grief, 41 direct reports! Who does it that early in your career?

I mentioned previously the impression I got at the Infantry School of a statue of a soldier carrying his rifle in his left hand with his right hand raised over his head, and the inscription, "Follow Me." In all the classroom lessons and all the field exercises and all the various training that we went through over the months at Fort Benning, to this day the biggest impression is that statue. The statue is inspirational in any case, but it spoke particularly to me because of my determination as young man in his first job - to learn how to be followed and how to be seen as a leader.

It matters not how many direct reports you have or how many people work with and for you, but as a leader your mantra is a very simple one. It is inscribed on the base of that statue. Nobody is interested in hearing how difficult your day was and how many things that you started and how many things you didn't get done. All they want to know is what you want them to do and when you want it done. Do you lead from the front or do you lead from the rear?

That's not to say you should have an inspirational statue erected in the reception area of your offices, although in some organizations that might be a good idea. No, what I'm saying is that the people who work in your organization hunger for meaning, and you should think about ways to help them find it and to gain their respect.

With "Follow me" echoing in my head, I went off to my first military assignment to a place called Fort Polk, Louisiana. I won't dwell on the geography or on my life as a bachelor 60 miles away from a civilized community, but in a real sense this was a new beginning, a new chapter, and a new day with a finish line that kept moving. Dealing with change has many forms. Your day can be disrupted by a phone call or any number of interruptions that can throw you off course. How often during the course of a day do you find yourself putting down what you're working on because an email message clicked onto your computer, or the phone rang, or somebody came into your office and asks, "Are you busy?" Sometimes you are never again able to pick up what it was you put down to deal with the interruption. More often than not, people are coming at you from every direction, now compounded by cyberspace.

In that first military assignment I was determined to ensure that not only did I do the best possible job, but that I would be decisive and that no task would be left undone. Sometimes it could be argued that those tasks were not necessarily done in a manner that those higher up would completely approve of. I recall in one of my earlier efficiency reports a statement appeared to the effect that "Lieutenant Arnhym tends to make snap judgments." Well, they didn't understand I was a West Point graduate, I'd been to the basic infantry officer's class at Fort Benning, Georgia, so I knew what had to be done, and I just did it. If that were a snap judgment, I would have to ask, "What's wrong with a snap judgment?"

After seeing that in my efficiency report, I decided the next time I got an order I would ponder for a few moments before I would issue my decision, and then I would proceed. In my next efficiency report it read, "Lieutenant Arnhym responds well to correction." Well, frankly, all I really changed is that I didn't issue my orders and make my decisions quite as quickly, but I at least gave the appearance of thinking a little bit. Sometimes appearances do matter.

Using Gatekeepers

We are a long way from the days when we had a gatekeeper to protect us from the interrupters. Today, there are so many interruptions that, irrespective of how hard I try and how diligent I may be, I'm not able to make decisions as quickly as I would like, much less get those things done that I felt were important in the first place. What I've done is program my PC so that I only receive messages when I hit "send/receive." My routine is when I get back to my desk from wherever, I check all of my voicemail messages and return them. Then I look at any hard mail and deal with that. Third, I look at my computer, hit "send/receive," let it kick out 30 (or 40, or 50) messages, and begin dealing with them. But here's the catch. I have programmed my PC in such a way that the only way a message is going to interrupt my thinking and my actions is if I consciously hit the "send/receive" button. In other words, I don't deal with email messages until I choose to deal with them. My PC is an automated gatekeeper, and it does not interrupt me.

My thinking is pretty simple, I will have answered all of those questions up to the point that I got behind my desk, I will have reviewed the mail, and I will have been responsive. After that, it's time for me to take control and take a look back and ask myself what is it I'm supposed to be doing today. Where is it written that you have to allow every interruption to interrupt? This singular fix, not unlike the old days, when we had gatekeepers, and you could issue an order: "I cannot be interrupted" or "I'm in a meeting." The latter of course was bogus, but everybody accepted it because everybody understood the need to get control of some part of your day.

More often than not, those voicemail messages, that email message, or that interruption during the course of your proceeding through your calendar or to-do list brings change of some sort with it. Change can take many forms and, needless to say, can have many impacts. One of the reasons (or maybe excuses) for not attending to that particular project or task on your to-do list is because you think that the situation is going to change.

When I was assigned to Fort Riley, Kansas as the Aide to the Commanding General, one day my boss asked me to research the Post regulations in response to a question that he had been asked. As I was fighting my way through the pages of this laborious, and don't have to tell you outdated, document, what amazed me in there was a statement that said, "Officers are enjoined not to shoot buffalo from the BOQ [Bachelor Officer Quarters] windows." It occurred to me that when General Custer left for the Little Big Horn, he was on his horse and probably looked at his Chief of Staff and said, "Chief, don't change a thing until I get back."

The Importance of Focus

As a result of what I do today, I have innumerable breakfast and lunch meetings, and what I've found out in some of the clubs is that the cooks generally have the buffet line with salads and soups and whatever, on the line by 11:00 a.m., and in some cases as early as 10:30, in anticipation of their lunch crowd. What was actually going on here was that they were just in a hurry to finish. I would note that those things, which were supposed to be cold, were warm and those that were supposed to be hot were cold. It leaves open the question of where their focus was. This is the same situation I encountered at Fort Ord, California, where I reduced the incident statistics by making the cooks prepare the food closer to the time it was to be eaten. I'm proud I was an agent of change then. Today, I am just a consumer of cold warm food and warm cold food. There is a limit to what I can change and when I draw a line in the sane – we just have to be sure to pick our battles.

What I learned back at Fort Ord was that performance must be aligned with the task at hand. For the cooks at the base, the task at hand was not to get cleaned up and get home early. The task at hand was to fulfill the need of the soldiers who required a wholesome and satisfying

157

meal. At the clubs where I have lunch and breakfast, the cooks are not finishing what they started because they have lost sight of the task at hand. The focus was on them, not the soldier. When you see this situation in business, it is a focus on the employee and not the customer.

The kind of change that I'm addressing in this particular chapter is not a change in ground rules. I am talking about a change of direction, to a course that takes you away from your plan, and a course where you find yourself either uncomfortable or unable to complete what you were doing, before you changed to take on a different task. It is how you deal with change and get back on plan that I want you to think about as you read these stories.

I mentioned before that at one point in my career I was assigned as the Aide-de-Camp to the Chief of the Joint Military Assistance and Advisory Group in Korea. This was post Korean War at the end of the 50's. My boss, a two-star General, worked with the Korean Joint Chiefs of Staff, the head of their Army, Navy, Air Force, Secretary of Defense, our Ambassador and various other leaders in South Korea. While we were there, there was a *coup d'état*, a civilian government had been in place and was failing, and a two-star Korean General who commanded one of their divisions near the de-militarize zone between North and South Korea engineered a *coup d'état*. By virtue of my job, I had gotten to know him - not well, but I knew him. As you would expect, subsequent to the coup, US forces were told to remain in their compounds and to limit communications with members of the South Korean government until direction had been established, authenticity had been assured, and that our State Department was convinced that the new leadership was in fact in the position to take leadership of South Korea.

158

Fortunately, the coup and the various military actions only lasted a couple of days and relative quiet was established very quickly.

This was ever so crucial given the tenuous nature of relationships between North and South Korea, and the fact that a truce agreement had been in effect since July of 1953, a military threat was uppermost in everyone's minds, and therefore any governmental instability was a path that we could ill-afford to go down. Finally, directives began to flow from the State Department, the Defense Department, Department of the Army, and various others that we could move ahead, albeit cautiously, in establishing relationships with the new government and their leadership. By definition, my boss was very much involved in the process.

The unexpected happened when the new President, who was assassinated some years later (today his daughter is the President of South Korea), decided that he was going to have a reception at the Presidential Palace and invite US and UN leadership to this event. This early after the coup made that problematic. However after multiple conversations and an exchange of messages, we were cleared and good to go. I went with my boss to the reception, and it was almost like a high school dance with the guys on one side of the room and the girls on the other side. Only this time, it was the South Korean folks on one side of the room and United Nations, US military, and various others on the other side. Communication was, at best, strained.

I was a Major at the time and who knows what compelled me to do it, but I walked up to the President, a former two-star General in the South Korean army, congratulated him and then said, "I really want to thank you. How in the world did you ever find out that today was my birthday? And here you're having all these folks over to wish me a happy birthday. What a cool thing."

Well, that threw him back about three paces but he was pretty quick on his feet, he called his aide over, who goes rushing over to the South Korean band and they start playing "Happy Birthday." This absolutely broke the place apart. Was this a foolish act on my part? Absolutely. But at the end of the day, it was about dealing with change, a change in government, a change in attitudes, in perceptions, and certainly in trust. It wasn't planned, but I like to think it acted as a transitional step to building a relationship with the new government. We could ill-afford to have a government in chaos facing a threat from the North Koreans. I can assure you that that was not on my punch list at the beginning of the day, but clearly another indication of a change in direction. Needless to say, my boss asked me "what did you just do?"

Three Rapid Changes

A change in culture, or a change in personnel can have the same impact. After I had served for over 20 years in the Army, I was asked to head up a small consulting company. What we did was market research, general marketing, marketing planning, and educational technology. The Electro-Optical systems division of Xerox in Pasadena, California hired our consulting company. They subsequently won the contract. One thing led to another and I found myself being offered a job by the Electro-Optical Systems division of Xerox, You will remember I was in Orlando, Florida at the time.

This was a major cultural change for me. In a short space of time, I found myself out of the Army, heading up a small consulting company in Orlando, Florida, and now in corporate America. When my world changed, I learned that I could not expect the new world to adjust to me. I had to adjust to it. I learned one thing very fast: don't decorate my office with my military awards. I sensed that this was too intimidating and I had to prove myself as equal to the task and able to work in a narrow space first. The reality is that this was a time in the history of our country where veterans were not looked upon with great favor.

I also learned that it's fundamentally necessary to know your people while you're making the adjustment. When I arrived as the new CEO in Beverly Hills, I made it a point to immediately visit every board member. But if you know what a Chamber of Commerce is, you know it has a constituency: its members. I wanted to get to know them, and at the same time I wanted them to know me. My mission was simple – listen. I also made a point to visit each board member and I never took my car if I could avoid it. I walked, and along the way I would stick my head in various businesses and introduce myself. Now I knew that I had my desk piled with stuff, there were reports to look at and papers that had to be signed, and staff members that wanted my time, and that I was the new kid on the block and all that good stuff. But, I had a number of things I needed to know in order to be effective in my job:

- What was each board member's agenda?
- What were they thinking?
- What was important to them?
- What needed to get done first?

- Do the above, and still make time for my new staff.

I had similar questions for the members. It wasn't just simply about my running through my checklist and satisfying myself with the fact that I had gotten everything done that I thought that I had to get done by the time I went home at night. That wasn't it. I was being measured by whether I did those things that each of my board members felt was important and by whether I did those things that the membership felt was important. These were people who were working hard to make their businesses prosper in a very difficult economic environment. In the big picture, my checklist counted for very little to anyone but me.

As a CEO of a Chamber of Commerce, and ultimately heading four of them in California, I would always find out what was number one in terms of priority to the Chairman of the Board and then make it my number one on my list. Because, of course they knew that I had a list of my own and things that I had to get done. Let me be clear – I've used a number of examples from my military career and certainly from my combat experience. Why? Those lessons learned were fully transferrable, but with a significant competitive advantage or differentiator: focus, discipline, and the ability to lead people. I was very careful to listen and slow to talk about my military career unless asked. As I built the relationship, I was more open to talking about my career, but only after they had exhausted themselves with their story. Frequently, I was asked if I carried any strange habits, like ducking if I heard a loud noise or being spooked by the sound of a helicopter. I have to admit to one bad habit. When it rains, I tend to take off all of my clothes, grab a bar of soap, and run outside. Try living in the jungle for a year and you will get the idea. So, when I started everything, I made sure it included their tasks and mine. At the end of the day I had to take a look around and say, "Did I do those things that the Chairman expected me to do? Did I do those things that the members expected me to do today?" It was only after answering those questions could I ask, "Did I do those things that I knew I had to get done?"

Working with People

As a CEO of a Chamber of Commerce, I had to conduct and attend monthly mixers. Needless to say those took me away from my desk and that long line of things that I knew I had to get done but, while I may have thought of the mixers as disruptive, they were part of the deal. Each one forced me to take a change of direction during the course of an already busy and complicated day full of appointments and meetings. Mixers are one of the things that every Chamber prides itself on. In these events, they bring members of the business community to somebody's place of business once a month to introduce that business and increase interaction between the members. The bottom line is that every member expects that membership in the Chamber will translate into business – the facts are that they have to be pro-active and engaged for this to happen.

Beverly Hills being what it is, after every mixer I could expect a call from one or more members of my board or various other people within the community from various levels of responsibility, and I'd get chastised because I didn't talk to them the night before at the mixer. After several such chastisements, I finally came up with an answer. I said, "You know, the mixers last two hours. That's 120 minutes. I make it a point not to spend more than two minutes with any one person so that I can be there for as many folks as I can. I managed to talk with roughly 60 people per event. By the way, where is it written that you could not come up to me?" I don't have to tell you the impact of that discussion.

This inevitably raises an interesting point: when you're out at an event of some kind or another, how many people do you interact with? If you're at a table for dinner, do you go around the table and introduce yourself to the other seven or nine? Or do you just drop down in your chair and hope that the thing will just be over soon? I can't tell you how many key officials in government and elsewhere that I've walked up to, introduced myself and have had absolutely delightful conversations and in most every instance was welcomed because nobody wanted to come up to talk to them without wanting to have something.

While I was in Beverly Hills, it came time for my performance evaluation and the executive committee graciously let me know that they thought I was doing a good job. However, I had not made one very important cultural change: I was still wearing a sport jacket and slacks, which was pretty common when I was the CEO of the Palm Springs Chamber of Commerce, but they let me know that the expectation was that I should be wearing dark suits. I looked at them and said, "Well, that's great. Those suits do not come inexpensively, and I'd be very happy to comply if you guys would give me some sort of a wardrobe budget."

As it turned out, one of our members was the general manager of Saks Fifth Avenue and (not unlike *Wheel of Fortune* where they have a plan for how they dress the main players) Saks became my official wardrobe of source. They made sure that I was properly attired in dark suits. At the end of the day, it is always about people and their impressions of you. It is how relationships get started, but also may frequently require you to change something about yourself or about your demeanor.

Learning to Observe

An interesting sidebar on dealing with change is how something that can throw you off plan. How your day starts and what happens during the course of it is frequently impacted by something that has caused you to shift or change from what you're working on and moving on to something else. I have disciplined myself over several careers to focus on change and being alert to it. That discipline is probably what has made the difference for me in my ability to know when to make that shift or how to get back to where I was in the first place. Too frequently you can get going down one path, something happens and gets you going down a second path, something else happens and you're on a third path, and you can't figure out how to get back to where you started.

Here's something about dealing with change that generally goes unremarked. You can't deal with change if you don't see it. You need to be a careful observer. In combat, you're trained to look around you and in front of you at first light to see if something has changed. If there is a change, then that means that you better take another look at your plan of action for that day and be prepared for something that you perhaps did not contemplate before. I've carried that lesson forward with me in so many ways. When I walk into somebody's office I will look around for something that has changed in his or her office, or something that has recently appeared. It could be a picture of their family, it could be a trophy, or it could be something that was presented to them. The office could have been painted; they could have rearranged it, anything. This kind of observation has two benefits. First, it gives you additional information about the person you're dealing with, which is always useful. Second, it tells that person that you care enough about them to notice changes they have made in their work area. It always opens up the dialogue, and I'm never disappointed by the results. The ultimate result is that they are more open, and the conversation tends to be more relaxed, because they realize that you are there for them, not they for you.

While I was serving as the CEO of the Pasadena Chamber of Commerce, I was invited as a distinguished guest to fly to Colorado Springs and, among other places, visit the US Air Force Academy. One of the first things that I noticed is that in all three of the chapels, the US flag was improperly displayed. It was on the wrong side of the pulpit.

As a side comment, I want to mention that it's characteristic of the graduates of our various military academies to be supportive of one another 364 days out of the year. It's only on one day when we're playing football that all that falls apart and we become very competitive. Trust me, the day after the bond is solid and unbroken. It is being bound and having loyalty that shaped graduates helps to better understand teamwork and to deal with change.

It's not long after that visit that I am hosting the Superintendent of the Air Force Academy for dinner in Pasadena because he's going to be the guest speaker at a major event that we're holding. I could not resist the opportunity to tell him, all in good fun, that as a West

Point grad I noticed at the Air Force Academy that the US flag in all three chapels was improperly displayed. He could not get back to the Air Force Academy fast enough to gnaw on his Chief of Staff. He made sure that all the flags were moved to their proper locations.

Different Ways of Doing Business

We all need to be attentive of our surroundings. We need to be constantly looking for something that has changed or has changed the dynamic or could alter the course of events for an otherwise well-planned day. The plan that you had at the beginning of the day may have been put together in isolation. You may be missing a number of facts, some activity, event, or some cultural shift or dynamic that's taken place in the workplace that can upset an otherwise pretty well thought out plan on your part. It may change the course of your life, or it may only get the flags moved.

As you know by now, I've had several major changes in my professional life: from Army to civilian, from small company to a large one, from a company to a Chamber of Commerce. From one Chamber of Commerce to another, each was equipped with a unique environment and business community. Each one of those changes had a significant impact on the way that I conducted business on a daily basis. It made a difference in terms of how I approached my to-do list in the early hours of the morning and how I viewed them at the end of the day.

After over 20 years of heading up four different Chambers in California, I made a family decision to move to Tampa, Florida in order to be closer to our two daughters and four grandchildren. That change was huge. I was leaving my comfort zone and a lot of people that I knew and a lot of people that I could turn to both personally and professionally. All of a sudden, I'm now in Tampa, Florida asking myself, "What am I going to do now?" Retirement wasn't even on the horizon.

I went on a networking rampage - not to collect other people's business cards, but to build relationships. This meant keeping a full schedule, a breakfast, and a lunch every day, which kept my calendar full for 30 days out. To this day, I maintain the same schedule. It also meant attending events and activities, as well as being seen as "being everywhere." Within a relatively short period of time I was approached with the opportunity to become a Chairman for Vistage, an international organization of over 16,000 executives worldwide. This position has given me the opportunity to work with over forty-five CEOs and senior executives.

Across the board, I'm finding that they all face the same issue that I faced – starting everything and finishing nothing. Great plans can start at the beginning of the day, but will find them being pulled in multiple directions during the course of a very busy and interrupted day.

Well, I did change direction, but I still face the same issues on a daily basis. I have all those things on my to-do list and at the end of the day, not all of them are done. I have learned no matter what changes happen, there are two things that always remain the same: you've got to prioritize, and you've got to protect quality time. You have to be flexible, not loose. If you're going to manage your time, first be respectful of the other person's time. Second, don't let them waste your time. Finally, avoid wasting your own.

Chapter 12

Changing Careers

There is one part of your professional life in which the problem of starting everything and finishing nothing doesn't even apply, and that's changing careers. Career change, when it is the result of a promotion or a new opportunity, means that what you started you really finished. You were at the top of your game, and it was time to go to the next level. You may have started everything but you found a way to finish by maintaining your focus on the priority tasks that kept you on the path to your major or priority goal. You managed the "interrupters," and you managed your time. You probably left behind a few unfinished projects, but the bottom line is you consistently got the job done.

When I graduated from West Point, we could hardly wait for that first salute. As I looked around at my classmates at graduation, I could see the pride in the eyes of the moms and the dads. Their children had graduated from the US Military Academy. We were filled with excitement as we looked back over four years of hard work and what we had finished, but not really, as it was just time for the next step and a career in the United States Army. I could hear parents asking their kids what was next. Were they focused on becoming a General? I was amazed when I

169

heard one of my classmates respond, "I want to be a First Lieutenant." He was looking out 18 months, not 25 to 30 years.

Where was your head on your first job? Did you have your eye on the corner office or on the office with a door? As my career evolved over 20 years, it saw me serving in multiple command capacities (at increasing levels), staff, plans, training, and operations. On balance, it was a very eclectic career. In every one of those capacities I accumulated a number of lessons learned, each built on the other. In two decades, there was one overriding principle: failure was not an option. Whatever I started, I had to finish, period! That principle has shaped my life in the Army, and when I left, it was for a whole new kind of job: a genuine career change. I had to do a forensic analysis of my skill sets and determine the strengths that would get me to my new finish line.

Needless to say, this was a huge decision to give up a culture that I loved and an Army that had given me countless experiences in locations literally all over the world. I don't have to tell you that my wife almost killed me. But, as I looked around, I noted that a number of officers were finishing their careers at the 30-year point, retiring and then going to a second job or a second career out of necessity. Maintaining their standard of living required income over and above retirement pay. I also noticed that many of them had taken on jobs that they approached with little or no enthusiasm and in which they found little fulfillment.

This troubled me as I looked at that landscape, and I said to myself that if someone should come along and offer me an opportunity, I should at least take a look at it to see if it was going to be the right fit for me. Failing that, and using an Army term, I was just going to continue to march. As it turned out, I was very fortunate. I didn't need to seek an opportunity; the opportunity sought me. A small consulting company in Orlando, Florida that was focused on marketing, community and public relations, and educational technology asked me to sign on. So I did, and along the way I found myself running a congressional campaign, chairing the Orange County Florida Bicentennial, and chairing the Orlando Centennial.

Goal #1: Customer Service

It was the Chamber of Commerce that crystalized my understanding that a successful career can involve starting everything and finishing nothing. In Chamber work, there's an expectation that you start a lot of things and pass each one on to a committee. The CEO of a Chamber of Commerce works at the pleasure of a Board of Directors. Each board member has his or her goal or project and wants to see it all done during their term typically, a minimum of three and a maximum of six years, if they are reelected. The board chair serves for one year, and they always come back with a goal or goals that they see as their legacy. It has to be accomplished in that framework of 12 months. I always made certain that the goal was of the chairman was my top priority. That's just simply good sense 101. The boss's goal is your number one goal.

In parallel, I established a relationship with the Chairman-Elect in an effort to build a relationship and to get an early start on understanding their goals, so I could begin planning how we were going to get there. When they became the Chairman, then their goal became my number one goal. My strategy was to meet or exceed that goal as soon as possible so that I could then refocus on meeting the goals of our directors and finally my own goals. My goals ran along the lines of growing the organization and filling the needs of the membership whom I saw as our clients; inherent, managing, motivating, training the staff, and - very importantly - in managing the budget. Understand that while a Chamber of Commerce is characterized as non-profit, that is for tax purposes and not the way you're going to meet payroll.

I saw the economic development function as being focused on attraction and retention of business, as well as a daily need to provide members with information, assistance, and promotion so that they could grow their individual businesses. Purely and simply, this was customer service. As the CEO of the Pasadena Chamber of Commerce, I made it a point to visit every committee meeting. I was careful not to divert attention from the volunteer chair or my staff member assigned to support that particular committee. But I needed to be plugged in. I was visible, and I was able to multiply my touches. While it did keep me from completing a number of tasks on my to-do list, it was simply good customer service, and it was effective. Did it impact my time and ability to finish tasks? Of course it did.

This was my first crack at the world of the Chamber of Commerce. I realized that my time was not my own and my agenda and priorities had to shift to the membership (i.e., customers) and obviously to the board of directors. Each member of the board had an agenda, albeit very often a hidden one. Getting to my to-do list came at the end of the day and more often than not before the day even got started. Candidly, many tasks got carried over to the next day. After almost seven years with the Pasadena

Chamber of Commerce I found that my job was becoming more cyclical and repetitive. There was no path to a greater challenge or high position, so I sought a new opportunity in a larger community. Ultimately, I looked at an opportunity that had surfaced as the CEO of the Long Beach Chamber of Commerce - a position that I was ultimately offered and accepted.

Party in a Phone Booth

I kept my membership in the Tournament of Roses and my links to good friends and associations that I had established while I was in Pasadena. To this day, I am a lifelong member of the Tournament of Roses and have fond memories of the Rose Bowl games, as well as my relationships with a lot of really fine people. My farewell from Pasadena was difficult at best. I joked that my farewell party would be held in a phone booth on Colorado Boulevard. As a matter of fact, what really happened is that the event was held at Ambassador College, the organizers put a phone booth out in front of the student union with a sign that read "Rolfe's Farewell Party" with arrows pointing to the student union labeled "Overflow." More than 700 people came.

It was a bittersweet moment, but once again I felt that it was time for me to move on. Long Beach presented its own set of challenges. It was not walk-able like Pasadena. The Chamber of Commerce was seriously in debt and losing members, which meant a different allocation of my time. There were so many things that I wanted to start but could not. Financial matters aside, they were looking to move their offices (just went through that in Pasadena). The *Queen Mary* and the Spruce Goose were major attractions, and they provided something that I did not have in Pasadena – a major tourist destination. As a

173

sidebar, when they brought the *Queen Mary* from Great Britain to Long Beach there were a number of unexpected obstacles.

The first was that the ship was wired for 220, and of course in the US, we've got 110. That created all sorts of chaos. The second is that as long as it was a ship, the applicable union was the Longshoreman Union, which was very high-priced, while the unions servicing the onshore hotels were the Teamsters. They found a way to get around this one by building a cement barrier around the ship, which ensured that it was locked securely to the land. At this point, it was no longer thought of as a ship, but as a hotel. The Spruce Goose, which is actually made of spruce but birch, offered many opportunities for meetings. It's highly visible from the air and any time if you're taking off or landing from LAX, you can look down and quickly identify Long Beach thanks to this very, very visible and major structure.

The combined ports of Los Angeles and Long Beach were a major asset and a magnet. The potential for greatness was clearly there and over the years that potential has, in fact, been realized. Like others, the Chamber had monthly networking breakfasts. I found that just doing a self-introduction ("my name is") was not cutting it and people were just not paying attention at those important networking functions, which were crucial to membership retention. Accordingly, I started a practice of adding a component where they had to identify their tagline. For many, this was foreign because they didn't have a tagline and so they were challenged to come up with one. One of the best taglines I heard came from the GM of a local mortuary. Her tagline was "It is better to know us and not need us, than need us and not know us." It could be

174

argued that that tagline could be applied to almost any business.

Life Can Change in an Instant

Other issues began to surface, which imperiled my ability to control my time, and in fact were major distractions. The Chairman wanted us to start publishing a magazine under the auspices of the Chamber, at a time of cost cutting and belt tightening. The net revenue projections notwithstanding, I felt that the risks were too high. While I was focused on belt-tightening, this project was suggested as an opportunity to jumpstart the revenue.

My concern was that at a time when the membership was already shrinking and somewhat gun-shy, while they were already buying tickets for events and activities, meeting increased dues, being asked to advertise in the directory, advertise on a map, this would be the straw that would break the camel's back. The Chairman had already insisted that I hire a personal friend to do the sales for this magazine project. The event was being held at Spruce Goose and, thankfully, there was an enormous turnout. In attendance was the salesperson for the magazine. Unfortunately, he got drunk, got into a fight with an attendee, and I was faced with one of the more difficult decisions as the CEO of the Chamber of Commerce. It was too visible and there was no way to hide it.

While being a drunk was one thing, getting into a fight with an attendee was another, so I fired him on the spot. This did not bode well with the Chairman, and I knew that this was going to imperil our relationship. My goals with the Chamber of Commerce were to increase membership, get us out of the red, and achieve financial stability. While I didn't exactly see my life flash before my eyes, I realized that this was a task that I was not going to be able to complete, at least in this environment. The good news is that the Palm Springs Chamber of Commerce, who were conducting a search for a new CEO, had already contacted me. This had come about via friends from Pasadena I had confided in, and who were frequent visitors to the desert.

I was both disappointed and relieved at the same time. I don't like to not finish but an exciting and new opportunity mitigated that disappointment. The welcome in Palm Springs made closing the Long Beach chapter the right thing to do.

Palm Springs was a different culture and clearly more laid back. Golf attire was the norm. They would shut down from May 15 to October 15 because it was just too hot, which I could see would interfere with my mission to make it a 24/7 world-class business destination. I was charged with growing the Chamber of Commerce and making it more relevant. A relationship with Sonny Bono, which grew over time, provided me with introductions to a number of celebrities in the entertainment industry. I created an annual event honoring celebrities, which incidentally carried over to Beverly Hills. We created a number of events and activities, all of which were intended to ratchet up the visibility of the Chamber of Commerce and energize the membership. Needless to say, all of this activity wreaked havoc with my to-do list. It was obvious that not everything was going to get done, which is a slippery slope by itself. So much of what you do in Chambers of Commerce is built around volunteers. The volunteer structure by itself can eat your time. There were days when I felt I was being nibbled by ducks.

Turning an Opponent into an Ally

I recall one individual who approached me to say, "You know some time I'd like to be the Chairman of the Board of the Palm Springs Chamber of Commerce. What have I got to do?"

I said something like, "Well, a good start point is for you to get active in the committee structure, and then once you're in the committee structure, strive for a position of responsibility, then shoot to become a vice chair and ultimately the chairman." As a matter of fact, when we start selecting potential members to serve on the Board of Directors, the first place we look is to the Committee Chairs. Once on the Board, you have to be a productive and participative member. At the same time, you strive to become a member of the executive committee and ultimately shoot for that top spot. Well, I helped this particular individual, and it wasn't too many years later when he, in fact, he became the Chairman of the Board of the Palm Springs Chamber of Commerce.

It turned out he had a hidden agenda, and somehow or another we found ourselves on opposite sides. I lost his support. The good news is that the other members of the Executive Committee did not see it the same way and sided with me. While it made for some sleepless nights, a lot of second-guessing, and a lot of tasks not done, I made it through his year. Then the improbable occurred. I had won his respect and ultimately his friendship. It's funny how that works.

It had been a very long time since my wife and I had taken a vacation, and we finally set our sights on going to Hawaii. Unfortunately, at the precise time that we picked for this vacation, the City Council was about to address an issue where they were going to remove the Visitors Bureau from the Chamber of Commerce and make it a separate entity essentially reporting to the city.

The budget implications were horrific and it would mean a loss of funds to the Chamber of Commerce, and a reduction in salary in my case. The moneys were just not there. We came up with all sorts of contingency plans and strong arguments why that should not occur. My board urged me to go on vacation anyway, and that they would deal with the City Council meeting. We got to Hawaii and as a second leg of our trip we went over to Maui. We had arrived at our hotel in Maui in the late morning when it provided me the opportunity to get on the phone and find out what the City Council had done the previous night. To my horror, the City Council had voted to strip the Visitors Bureau away from the Chamber of Commerce.

Aside from the financial impact there was an indirect impact. Potential visitors to our community would call the Visitors Bureau and ask for recommendations in terms of things to do, places to go, places to eat, and we would, needless to say, recommend them to Chamber members. This was huge for us. Without that, the call volume was going to go down and then many of our members, who had simply joined the Chamber looking for referrals, would then ask themselves the question about the value of the Chamber. I now had to deal not only with unhappy neighbors, but staff and program reductions - never mind the hit that I was going to take.

While I was in Palm Springs, the Governor appointed me to the California-Nevada Super Speed Train Commission. This was fascinating and challenging, as well as an opportunity to be a part of a project that I at least hoped would have a significant impact on California and certainly on the desert community. Of all the projects that I was involved in, this was probably the most fascinating and fulfilling. It also got me thinking out of the box and at a critical time. Additionally, I was urged to run for County Supervisor. After I decided to do it, I found myself running against three mayors who had pretty well established constituencies. It was probably not the smartest thing to do because along the line I broke some china. There was a real question as to whether I was able to accomplish my responsibilities as the CEO of the Chamber of Commerce and concurrently run for political office, even though I went to great lengths to separate the two, to work the extra hours, and to make sure that all of my tasks were done. You will recall my earlier comment that being a CEO is not unlike being in combat. There will always be someone shooting at you.

Beverley Hills – Right Place, Right Time

Maybe they thought I was going to win and I was on my way out or that I was looking for a better opportunity. Candidly, the bigger issue was that I ultimately could not live on a reduced salary, never mind that we had a great home and a lot of good friends. Once again I could not finish all the things that I had started but on balance isn't that really the way it is. You start a lot of things. You finish a lot of things, but you can't finish them all. The good news is that using my celebrity contacts I was asked to apply for the CEO position of the Beverly Hills Chamber of Commerce. I accepted that position and realized instantly that I had a better fit in a faster-paced metropolitan community, as opposed to a desert community and a tourist destination.

I would add also that the folks in Beverley Hills went out of their way to make me feel welcome and to make it feel like home, which totally runs contradictory to so many opinions of Beverly Hills as being a tad egocentric. I started with a goal to meet with each member of the board, members of the City Council, as many of the key leaders and key business owners as I could. I cast my to-do list off to the side and rather than immersing myself behind closed doors, buried in budget, staff going over policies and procedures, I got out there instantly. All the things that had to be done internally were on my night list. My days became extremely long, but I felt building the relationships early on and listening to members of the Board of Directors and community leaders was an imperative if I was going to get the job done. This was, in fact, another turnaround. My charge was to increase market share on the West Side because it was found that Beverly Hills was losing market share to the West Side of Los Angeles, to increase membership, and to get the Chamber of Commerce on a strong financial footing. It was the same charge given to almost any new Chamber of Commerce CEO.

I did not endear myself with the volunteer CFO, who was beyond hands-on (If the toilet broke, he had just the right plumber.), but others rallied around me. At least in that instant, I knew who was shooting at me. The chairman in particular was extremely supportive and each successive Chairman was beyond supportive of my efforts and ultimately each became a friend. The key always was to focus on their goals not mine and to make sure that in the eyes of the board of directors, the membership, and community that they had a legacy that they could move on, that they could trumpet as they handed over the gavel to their successor.

We were able to right the financial ship and grew the Chamber of Commerce to a size that exceeded that of the Los Angeles Chamber of Commerce, which was a little bit of an embarrassment to them. Along the way, I established a strong partnership with the Iranian-American community. Many Iranians were in retail, and they were a vital part of the community. It made absolutely no sense to have two camps each with the same goal and the same objective. I was also able to reach out the College of Business at UCLA and establish a partnership with them. Although the neighboring community to UCLA is Westwood, Beverly Hills became their partner, and ultimately I used this same approach in linkages with legislators in Sacramento.

I also visited our congressman from Beverly Hills, a Democrat who had been in office for a number of years. Through the Mayor and City Council, I was able to arrange a meeting with him. When I got to his office he asked me, "What are you doing here? We've never had anybody from the business community come in here. Never mind a Republican."

I made it clear that rain or shine he was still our representative, and I was representing the business community, and we just had to talk to each other – end of story. While we didn't always agree, but we established a relationship and mutual respect won the day.

I think the Beverly Hills Chamber of Commerce became one of the high points of my career in the world of Chamber of Commerce. Candidly, I fit the culture but more important I had a trunk full of lessons learned and it was time to put that learning into play.

The Decision to Go to Tampa

During this entire period in Beverly Hills, both our daughters and grandkids were living in Florida. I did not want our grandkids to not know their granddad and their grandmother, so at some point there was not really going to be a real finish to my time in Beverly Hills. The only things left to start were relationships with the grandkids. In my case, I did not really have a relationship with my grandparents. They were just pictures on the piano. I decided that we had to make the leap, which meant leaving a huge network of friends and a California lifestyle that I loved. As I mentioned previously, I told my California friends, who shared my belief that any place outside of California was likely to be jungle wilderness, that I had become nostalgic for Vietnam.

But the Vietnam comparison was a joke, as moving to Florida was a family decision and speaks to work-life balance – our daughters, their husbands, and our grandkids trumped my California lifestyle. After almost eight years in Beverley Hills, we moved to Tampa to start again. As a precursor to determining just exactly where we were going to live, and those who live in Tampa will understand the terminology, you really weren't with it unless you lived south of Kennedy, which is a major street running through Tampa. We opted to live in a community north of town in what is called Tampa Palms in a small-gated community. The reason that we selected that particular community is that it was wide open, no overhead wires. I could have the same sense of space that I enjoyed in California, although I didn't have the view anymore. Trust me, this was a bummer. For years we had been blessed with seeing the city sights in the distance and from a very quiet neighborhood.

Our new neighborhood was gated so we had security and, with early selection of a lot, our property was pretty well protected so I could take some of the California lifestyle with us. Of equal importance, there was an opportunity to become a member of a Country Club that had both golf and tennis, which would provide us with an entry point to establish new relationships. I was really not ready to retire, which in my definition is doing what you want to be doing. I decided that I was a long way from being finished. There was a drum inside of me that told me I was not finished. That there was more to do, that there was something that I could be doing and a way for me to give back. I was looking for a way that I could share my lessons learned and my experiences so that others would not make the same mistakes that I had made.

So, the finish line moved out a little bit further as I went on a networking rampage looking for that perfect fit. Pretty soon I knew a ton of people, but they had no idea what I did or what I was looking for. This forced me to take another look and redefine myself as to what I did. Clearly, what I had been doing was heading up Chambers of Commerce for over 20 years and a military career that spanned over 20 years and as a Program Manager for an engineering company and, of course, heading up my own small consulting firm. While I was looking to replicate that, the improbable occurred - I was tapped on the shoulder by someone who said, "I think that you should consider becoming a chairman for Vistage."

At that time it was called TEC, which stood for The Executive Committee and the name has since been changed. It struck me that as I look back at all the things that I had started and may not have finished nor completed to my satisfaction, this was the opportunity to replay the lessons learned to the CEOs and senior executives I was privileged to work with. Each of them faced the same challenges I faced. Each struggled to get through their to-do lists and competing priorities. I realized that life in the business world does not always have a finish line. As I have, everywhere that I have been, I worked to establish relationships.

How to Enter a New Community
When I joined the Chamber of Commerce in Tampa, I figured out that the key was to become an active member and not a passive one. I noted that there was no Veterans Day event in the City of Tampa or in downtown Tampa in particular. There were various Veterans Day activities around the community but nothing actually in the downtown area. Two of us took on that task and that was to build an event to observe Veterans Day in downtown Tampa. We sponsored it. We planned it. We executed it. I can happily report that that is now a standing event and part of the program of activity for the Tampa Chamber of Commerce. Over my various careers, and certainly in my Chamber of Commerce work, I maintained a close link to the military community to be as supportive as I possibly could. That link made it feel more like home and was a reminder of my love for my military career, specifically MacDill Air Force Base, with members of all services and branches.

When we moved to Tampa and into a new community, I saw things that had not been done that should be done and I realized that they weren't going to get done. I could not stop myself and I wound up as the President of the Homeowners' Association in a community called Windsor and Tampa Palms in Tampa, Florida. This was not an entirely new experience for me. When we lived in

Washington, D.C., I was President of the Homeowners Association. I guess that has been a pattern through all my various careers. I have seen things that were started and not finished, and something inside of me said that I needed to take that one on.

Maybe it's because I have no quit in me, but I think that I will never truly finish. Never mind what gets in the way. I mentioned in an earlier chapter about how much I hate it when I'm in a restaurant, partway through a meal, and a server asks, "Are you still working on that?" What does that mean? Why would they want me to regard my visit to their restaurant as work? Why not ask, "Are you still enjoying your lunch?"

In my careers, situations have repeated themselves over and over again. It's only the people that change, and to a lesser extent, the circumstances and the geography. Multiple careers have been a blessing.

I have been blessed with any number of awards, plaques, and citations, which I keep in my man cave or my home office - they are a reminder to me that I may have started a lot of things but I finished a lot of things as well. The walls are completely filled. I have no place to put another plaque or a citation. If I were to get another one, something has to come down. Over and over again, my wife has again suggested that since we moved into the house 14 years ago it's time to paint my office. My answer is a flat no. There is no way that I could figure out how to get all this stuff back up on the wall again. That is one task that I considered finished and I'm not going to start it again, yet it inspires me to continue to look for things that need to be done, for ways to give back and to make a contribution. I think that's what I've been looking for all along.

When people ask me and I ask myself, when are you going to retire? When are you going to be finished? My answer is very simple: I am retired because, to me, that means I'm doing what I want to do. It also means starting a lot of new things and hopefully being able to finish them.

Chapter 14

Getting It Done

You may have noticed that Chapter 13 is missing – Well, I started it, but I couldn't quite finish it.

What keeps you from finishing? While there are always other factors and other issues that can get in the way, more often than not, it's a person who became the obstacle. Maybe they won't make a decision. Maybe they don't agree with you. Maybe they aren't doing the job as you expected. The reasons vary with situations and personality types, but it's generally people that stand between you and what you want to accomplish.

The move of the Army-Navy Game was a good example of a continuum of people that were opposed to the idea at every level. Convincing them was a task in itself. Once it was a given, the rush was on for tickets and requests for VIP. seats for events – some I was never able to convince.

Giving up is not a part of my genetic make-up, nor should it be yours. The bottom line is, don't give up. Just simply get it done.

As the CEO of Chambers of Commerce in Pasadena, Long Beach, Palm Springs, and Beverly Hills, I found that I had to navigate seemingly insurmountable obstacles to achieve a successful outcome.

I moved the Army-Navy Game from Philadelphia to the Rose Bowl in Pasadena. They said it couldn't be done. I moved UCLA football from The Coliseum to the Rose Bowl. They said it couldn't be done. I chaired organized Bicentennials for both Orange County, Florida and the Centennial for Orlando. They said it couldn't be done. My advice is that if they say it can't be done, you should think again.

The key in the case of the Army-Navy Game was gaining support from those that had the most to gain. Those obviously were the Athletic Directors from the US Military Academy and the US Naval Academy. Both of these individuals were class acts and if anything inspired me to keep on going, it was these two gentlemen. As often as people are your greatest obstacles, they are your greatest source of support.

Both of these men saw the need to improve attendance of the game. Both of them saw the need to raise the visibility of Army and Navy football before the public because, after all, the Army-Navy Game is America's game. I know a lot of other games try to claim that phrase, but it belongs to the Army-Navy Game.

Both of those Athletic Directors supported me continuously throughout both the planning and the execution. The both of them were a source of energy and inspiration. There was no way that I could let them down or give up.

Clearly I knew my head was on the line as a West Point graduate, but as any graduate of West Point or Annapolis will tell you, there is a strong bond between members of the Army and members of the Navy. Mutual support was a given, and they became my army of one to get it done. Admittedly, there were some members of both the Army and the Navy who did not buy in. I did not have time for skeptics and naysayers, not unlike a bad client, and moving ahead was the path I followed. Needless to say, they re-appeared when we were working to call in pledges under very challenging circumstances. They were among the first ones to the lifeboats. What they did now know is that teams stayed on board, determined to get to finish.

Leveraging Relationships

The next step in the process was for me to leverage those relationships to win the support of key decision makers. My premise and has always been once the decision makers are in place, and the decision is made – now, get on with it.

There is a saying, "Lead, follow, or get out of the way." I found it necessary to apply all three. In retrospect, I probably had to coach more people than I would care to think about to simply get out of the way. To do that, I had to lead. I had to be decisive and I had to get people to follow.

There are five principles that I would share with you that are crucial to getting it done:

- Stay focused. Be fully present and decisive.
- Be time-sensitive, set limits and deadlines, and know when the task has to be accomplished.

- Be quick on your feet, make decisions quickly and be responsive to the doubters and convert them to followers.
- Leverage relationships.
- Always have a Plan B. I cannot overemphasize the necessity for a plan B.

As a young man in high school in my first attempt to get into West Point, I was in first alternate position and, to my chagrin and disappointment, the principal appointee (the guy in front of me got the appointment) and I had to wait for another time. In other words, I had no Plan B... at least then.

I spent a year after that exploring every possible alternative to going to the military academy and at the same time, to finding every possible path that might get me there. A year later, I had been accepted at a number of colleges and universities in California and concurrently had appointments for both West Point and Annapolis. Needless to say, my first choice and only choice in my mind was to go to West Point. The important point here is that I had a choice. I now had a Plan B.

The Plan B approach certainly came in handy when moving the Army-Navy game. Also, in that particular instance, every time I ran into a people roadblock, I found somebody else that I could gain their support and leverage their relationships, which speaks to principle number four.

People often confuse networking with building relationships. To me, building a relationship simply means that there is continuous contact and not simply a business card that winds up in your breast pocket.

If you're like me, unless you have made a note on the back of the card as to where you met this person, some of the circumstances, and a little bit about that person, you may turn that card over a week later and realize to your horror that you can't remember anything about the person. The so-called networking opportunity is lost.

I would urge you to do what I have always done and that is to follow up after a networking event, with all those business cards that wind up on your desk, and let them know that you value the opportunity to meet them and applaud something that stands out in your mind about that person. It could be as simple as acknowledging their family or something that they've accomplished.

This is what relationships are all about. Through my contacts at West Point, I was able to meet counterparts at Annapolis. Both Athletic Directors facilitated introductions for me to the Academy Superintendents, who are like College Presidents. They are responsible for the training and the discipline within the Corps of Cadets and the Brigade of Midshipmen. I was also able to get access to the Dean of each of the academies, whose support was crucial because after all, they would be less than supportive with the idea of Cadets and Midshipmen missing a day of class.

Eventually Everyone Signs On
I must add at this juncture that once a decision had been made to move the game to the Rose Bowl in Pasadena, both command teams from the Military Academy and Naval Academy could not have been more supportive or more helpful. This made a huge difference and once again, kept me going and kept me from giving up when I ran into one obstacle right after another.

As the CEO of the Pasadena Chamber of Commerce, I had the charge of bringing additional business opportunity to Pasadena. I realized the city had physical assets that were being underutilized: the Rose Bowl. I was looking for other opportunities beyond the move of the Army-Navy Game to Pasadena where even a greater use can be made of this magnificent 104,000-seat facility. If you have ever visited or at least seen pictures of it, you know that it is the crown jewel of the San Gabriel Valley.

I saw UCLA as that opportunity. The Los Angeles Rams were a dominant force in the Coliseum where they had been playing their football games, and the University of Southern California was the other, which left UCLA on the third rung of the ladder. In addition, UCLA was playing in enemy territory in downtown Los Angeles - a fact that did not go unnoticed to the thousands of UCLA (Bruins) fans in the Los Angeles area and beyond.

It struck me that if UCLA were to move their home games from the Coliseum to the Rose Bowl in Pasadena, which could be at least five or six games a year that this could prove to be an enormous win for Pasadena. That number of games has obvious financial benefits to the Rose Bowl and the surrounding community. The trick was to convince a lot of people that this was a great idea. In my head, the Rose Bowl was a huge asset and, for all practical purposes, only used once a year on New Year's Day.

The folks in Pasadena certainly bought into this idea, but it was not uncommon for me to hear that it can't be done and I might as well give up the idea. There were too many obstacles. Again, it wasn't about money, it was about people.

Based on relationships that I enjoyed in the city of Pasadena by virtue of my job, I was able to meet with the Athletic Director at UCLA. At that time, average season ticket holders were at 32,000-33,000, which was far below an optimum level for the athletic department at UCLA to gain the sort of revenue it needed to support the football program, never mind their other programs.

It was at that point that I started my discussions with the Athletic Director at UCLA where, in a proposal, I noted that it should be possible for UCLA to have an average season tickets sale exceeding 55,000 within five years.

Needless to say, those around me thought that I was out of my mind. Nevertheless, I began to gather as much statistical information as I could on attendance at UCLA football games in the Coliseum while, simultaneously, I had the opportunity to meet and enter into a dialogue with key leaders at UCLA.

Working Around a Major Obstacle

There was a slight hitch in all of this and that was that the Mayor of Los Angeles, who was a graduate of UCLA, was certainly not going to allow UCLA to move from the Coliseum in downtown Los Angeles to the Rose Bowl in Pasadena, unless over his dead body. Doesn't that sound a lot like the obstacle when the Secretary of the Navy whose home was Philadelphia, took a rather dim view of the Army-Navy Game moving from Philadelphia to the Rose Bowl? Isn't it wonderful how history tends to repeat itself?

What finally made the day and caused a decision to be made was the economics. Being able to tap a huge fan base in the San Gabriel Valley in close proximity to the

Rose Bowl provided compelling evidence and persuaded not only the Chancellor of UCLA but their entire team, their alumni groups and others, to overcome the objections of the Mayor of Los Angeles and support the move of the game to the Rose Bowl.

There was only one slight hitch in this. The decision was made in the spring and we were looking at the first football game being played in September of 1985. The task at hand was enormous because season ticket holders in the Coliseum had to have their unique seating arrangement transferred into a Rose Bowl venue. This by itself was a huge undertaking because the configurations were dissimilar, albeit they were still tied to a location based on the 50-yard line.

Fortunately, the Athletic Director at UCLA agreed to a concept where one of his Assistant Athletic Directors would be embedded in my offices during this transition period. It was my intent to establish a close line of communication to ensure that the move was not only smoothly executed, but that we would jointly conduct a major marketing effort to not only gain the support of the existing 33,000 seat and ticket holders, but get moving towards our ultimate goal of 55,000.

Everywhere I went I took the Assistant Athletic Director with me, to the point that he became a recognizable individual in the city of Pasadena. In that way, we extended the advertising campaign, as well as the communication by letter and by bulletin into a physical presence.

There is nothing more important than one-on-one, face-to-face. The end result was that we met our five-year goal at the kick-off game: 55,000 tickets. It could not have happened without a collaborative effort between my staff and the folks in the Athletic Department at UCLA.

As a sidebar, the UCLA coach at that time noted that the locker room for the home team was of course on the same side as the press box, and was the farthest from UCLA. He wanted to have UCLA's locker room as close to UCLA as possible, which meant of course moving it across the field.

Every step of the way, it was clear that if we were going to get it done we could not just give up. We had to keep pushing. But most importantly, there was a hard deadline that we had to face and that deadline was obviously kick-off of their first home game in September.

Ever mindful that one of my charges as CEO at the Pasadena Chamber of Commerce was to exploit every possible idea with the view toward increasing business, I kept looking at other opportunities. Needless to say, the cooperation between the Pasadena Chamber of Commerce and the Pasadena Tournament of Roses had historical roots, which go back to the year 1890 when the first Tournament of Roses parade was held on the streets of Pasadena, then with decorated horses and carriages. Leveraging those relationships was truly the key to success.

Using All Assets
Several things struck me. The first is there was a requirement on the part of visitors coming to attend the Rose Bowl to spend at least three nights in the hotels prior to the Rose Bowl game itself, and there were limited options for them in terms of things to see and do in

Pasadena itself. It was pretty clear that there were ample opportunities in the Los Angeles area through the various attractions, museums, and so forth.

The Tournament of Roses already had a plan in place where the float decorators would allow the public on an admission basis to view the last couple of days of decorating some 50 floats that were to be in the Tournament of Roses parade. This was a fascinating process, which took several days and was a 24-hour per day effort with high school kids, church groups, and various others of providing the workforce to carefully put the various flowers on the all of the floats. The distinctive factor about the Tournament of Roses parade is that every surface has to be covered by something live.

Right after the parade on January 1st, float decorators are already at work designing the parade for the following year. This obviously includes the selection of flowers, as well as the type and the source, in a believable system to make sure that all of those flowers reach the decorating places in a timely fashion so that those floats can head out to their place on Orange Grove Boulevard on New Year's Eve. Not too many of us realize the logistics involved in making this happen. The float decorators and those that are working on those floats on New Year's Eve cannot give up, no matter how tired they may be. This is a wonderful lesson for young people before they enter the workforce, to understand the importance of not giving up, and that there are thousands of young people that were doing this work.

It is tiring and not as easy as one might think. There is a place for every single rose bud, for every single flower, every piece of bark, and every seed. It is meticulous work and it goes through the night. At that time of year, float decorating places are often pretty close to the freezing level. At one point, I was on the formation area committee for the Tournament of Roses as a volunteer responsible for band parade route. We had to be in place at 6:00 p.m. on New Year's Eve. The floats arrived and lined up two by two, stretching some distance. It's an extraordinary logistical exercise and almost as impressive as the parade itself. Fifty or more floats emerge from their various decorating places around Pasadena just after midnight to find their way into a line on Orange Grove Boulevard just before the start point at Tournament House on Orange Grove Boulevard.

There are separate streets that feed in the bands and the horses, and they join at a point just short of the starting line. From three directions things are making their way in: floats are coming from one direction, bands from another, and horses from still another. It magically starts at 8:00 a.m. on the morning of January 1st, rain or shine. I can assure you that no one is in a "give up" mode. They understand it has to get done, and it has to be done in time for that parade to start.

Thinking about this process as the Pasadena Chamber of Commerce CEO, I realized we had an unused asset, and that was the bands - some 25 bands from across the country and across the world that were carefully selected to participate in this magnificent event. It struck me that we could create an activity utilizing five of those bands and conduct a band festival on the 31st of December, which could potentially be a huge draw and another reason to keep people in the city of Pasadena, as opposed to looking for activities in the greater Los Angeles area.

The good news is that with those five bands, First Band Fest was a complete sell-out and a complete success. Then not too surprisingly, the folks at the Tournament of Roses took another look and said, "Wait a minute, those bands belong to us. Band Fest is a great idea. We're going to make it part of our schedule of events on a continuing basis."

Never mind that the Pasadena Chamber of Commerce sponsored the first event. And why was that? It was because there were a lot of folks that really didn't think that it was such a great idea, that it would never go anywhere. Who was going to come to see that other than the friends and families of the bands?

Based on the success of the band festival, it should be no surprise that the folks at the Tournament came up with another idea and that was to use some of the 250 horses that were going to be there. As a result, another event was created and continues to this day, and that's the Equestrian Event.

These two events are now enormously successful and so those that are coming for the Rose Bowl not only have the opportunity to see the floats being decorated, but they have the Band Festival and the Equestrian Event, and in addition, special events and activities are taking place at the Rose Bowl itself.

Beware Breaking China
We were approaching the possibility of broken china. The Chamber of Commerce might be seen as muscling in to or going beyond the mission and purpose of the Chamber of Commerce. It struck me that some visible activity, some event was necessary to cement the relationship between

the Chamber and the Tournament of Roses to ensure that it was about a partnership and not a competition.

Toward that end, I noted that once the Queen in Court had been identified, there were innumerable activities within the community and outside the community that focused singularly on the Queen and her Court. Probably one of the more fascinating was the Junior Chamber of Commerce with their black tie breakfast, which was the first opportunity for the Queen and her Court were introduced to the public.

With support from the Chamber's Board of Directors and concurrence from the Tournament of Roses, we put plaques in place naming past Grand Marshalls and Tournament Presidents, therefore creating a visual history.

In addition, with the support of my Board and Executive Committee, I proposed that we conduct a President's Luncheon to showcase and honor the President of the Tournament of Roses and give him the opportunity to tell the story of his year, his travels, his efforts to select bands, his decision to come up with the theme, and his decision regarding the Grand Marshal.

It also provided a preview of what to expect from the upcoming parade by way of new floats, new entries, and any personalities that would be appearing in the parade itself. This would solve the situation in which a float going down first Orange Grove Boulevard and turning on Colorado Boulevard, bearing a celebrity who would otherwise be a complete surprise.

All of these elements made for a most interesting event, which was immediately sold out. But very importantly, it solidified the strong and wonderful relationship that exists between the Tournament of Roses and Pasadena Chamber of Commerce. Of course, it helped that I was a working member and to this date I am still an honorary member.

There's a footnote. This parade traverses 5.2 miles with the floats ideally proceeding at 2.5 miles per hour and driven by a mini tractor completely hidden from view. Using these vehicles once a year is not a guarantee the system was going to work perfectly forever. Tow trucks were strategically placed along the entire route so that in the event of a float breakdown, a tow truck would magically appear and would tow the float the rest of the distance. More than a million spectators have no idea the tow trucks are there.

The some 25 bands that participate in the parade know as well that walking in a parade for 5.2 miles is a feat of endurance for a most of the high school kids, particularly when they have to carry and play an instrument. Practicing from a seat in their high school band room wouldn't be adequate preparation. After the parade, the bands would arrive for lunch and (in most cases) they can hardly wait to drop their instruments, take off their hats, and shed some article of clothing - one of these articles were typically their shoes. What they didn't realize is the minute they took off their shoes, their feet would expand, so when it was time for them to leave on their buses, you would see most of them carrying their shoes. Their feet would not fit in the shoes again. In the case of the bands as well as all those other participants, they had to stay focused. They had to be fully present. They had to understand that there was no giving up until they had gone the 5.2 miles and that float made the distance as well.

What It's Like to Volunteer

To conduct a parade of this magnitude, never mind its two-hour length, takes in the neighborhood of 800 Tournament of Roses volunteers.

You will recall that we had to report at 6:00 p.m. on New Year's Eve, and in the early morning hours we would then change into our white Palm Beach suits with red ties and white shoes. It was typically rather cold, and by then you had been standing for over 12 hours and nothing seemed to work. Your feet wouldn't move and your fingers weren't working. Yet, you were the face of the Tournament of Roses and you had to be there standing and smiling if your job was on the parade route.

There was a certain sense of magic to that uniform and a smiling member of the Tournament of Roses. All he or she had to do was to stand on the street facing the crowd, and they would magically obey and stay behind the line. We changed committees every two years, so the experiences were without limit.

In one of my assignments during the course of my active role in the Tournament of Roses, I was in that area where the floats go after the parade and can be viewed by the public. Several members of the tournament are assigned to each float and you are provided with a very detailed description of the length and height of the float, the type of every flower, every seed, every live item that's on that float, what the design is all about, who the sponsor is, because you had to be prepared to answer every kind of question that you can imagine from the public that was anxious to get up close to those beautiful floats.

If you think that something can't be done, remember the Tournament of Roses with its 25 bands, 50 floats, a veritable herd of horses, 800 volunteers, and a million spectators. If somebody can make that happen, there is hope for us all. Why do I close with my experience at the Tournament of Roses? Because it's about people making things happen. These examples, along with the move of the Army-Navy game, are annual and vivid reminders that if you start something, finishing will always depend on people. Your business will not grow or get through tough times without a motivated and well-led workforce. With the right attitude, skills, insight, and tenacity, anything can be accomplished. But at the end of the day, it's really up to you.

The Tournament of Roses parades is 5.2 miles long and with the exception of one turn, essentially a straight line. I know because I have walked it. Life is not like that. You are lucky if you go for a mile, never mind an hour, without an obstacle or interrupter in your path. It forces you to "decide to decide" which fork you will take, or maybe to decide that it "can't be done." You have been in my shoes through the pages of this book, and I that the lessons that I have learned have become light posts for you in business and in life in general. When I hit a roadblock, of which there were many, it only took my resolve to another level. And yes, the path is littered with these tasks, initiatives, even careers and jobs that were started but not finished. As I reflect back, however, in many cases my job was for all practical purposes done, and it was time for me to move on. In other cases, the other fork in the road opened up opportunities that I just did not see. I have always gone for the big audacious goal – that is just part of my DNA. I would like to tell you that in all cases I slayed the dragon. I didn't of course, but it was never for lack of trying. I have always had a full schedule and full agenda, but I also have protected time. Recall my statement on weekends when I strive to get from work-play-work to play-work-play. If you discipline yourself, you will know what to start and you will know that it isn't always easier if you do it yourself.

However, whatever you do, always start everything and finish...!

Afterword

An Insider's View of the Army-Navy Game

By COL (Ret.) Wesley Gilman

Next to Graduation and "R" Day, the Army-Navy Football Game is one of the biggest and most memorable times during the four-year tour at our Rockbound Highland Home. And in 1983, it was about to get even bigger and even more memorable.

I recall being summoned to a meeting at the Deputy Commandant's office early in my first year. I recall meeting COL (Ret.) Rolfe Arnhym there and, as I was about to learn, he had a plan. I am sure it was not his first plan, nor was it the largest one that he had ever developed. His plan was to move the Army-Navy Game and the Corps out to the Rose Ball in Pasadena, California. Now this was not your average "trip section," where maybe a couple of hundred Cadets and families go with the teams and cheer them on - this was the entire Corps, as well as all of the Midshipmen from the Naval Academy.

There were many people and organizations that worked extremely hard to ensure that COL Arnhym's plan came to fruition. My role was fairly small, but I recall doing my best to communicate to the Corps how this was all going to occur, although I am sure I could not visualize the real scope of the operation. As far as the lodging and the transportation went, I think we had 14-15 wide bodies lined up just for the Corps. Additionally, we would need 4000 "host families," and 2000 hotel rooms to house and feed the Cadets and Midshipman. I would continue to receive information through our TAC channels and through COL Arnhym's team, and then relay the information to the Corps. In addition to airplanes and host families, there were minor details to figure out, such as getting around the Pasadena/Southern California area, dress code for the days we would be out there, and linking up plans for the game. Some of this was similar to having the game in Philadelphia, but being 3000 miles away from West Point made it seem a bit more daunting.

I recall writing "updates" on the computer in my room - I believe that a then CPT Klinefelter (an instructor at the Academy) allowed the Brigade Commander and the 4 Regimental Commanders to have the first 5 desktops to ever enter into a room at West Point. I do not recall how we distributed the letters to the Corps, but I think it was something similar to delivering newspapers. The updates covered a sitrep on planning, timetables for departure and return, scheme of maneuver once on the ground (though I doubt I called it that at the time), as well as tips on etiquette and dress code. I seem to recall trying to ensure everyone had a sports coat, as I was not sure if a blazer would suffice.

One of my classmates reminded me of Disneyland - a rainy Disneyland that had closed just for us (the Corps) as an interesting memory. He also added that handing out kazoos before the game was a dumb idea, as Cadets found themselves in trouble for throwing 4000 kazoos on the field after Napoleon McCullum took the opening kickoff back for a touchdown.

Although the game was miserable for Army, the day itself was great and the post-game party was one to remember. For many of us, our fondest memories of that special weekend rest on the generosity that the Pasadena volunteer families showed us. They opened their homes, treated us like dignitaries, and they even loaned us their cars and heated their hot tubs for us in some cases. The Army may have lost the game, but in the end the Corps won - we gained so much more. Many of us met lifelong friends and some even met future spouses during that trip.

In the end, I believe much of the credit needs to go to COL Rolfe Arnhym. He had the vision, developed the plan, and made it work. This should not come as any surprise - he has been doing this for his entire life.

COL (Ret.) Wesley Gilman

Appendix

In The News

ARMY-NAVY

Friday, November 25, 1983 11:45 a.m. Rose Bowl Pasadena, California

City ready for Army-Navy game

Operation kickoff

Smooth sailing for Army-Navy game

9,000 Cadets, Midshipmen March on Pasadena

Opportunity, Money Surround Army-Navy Game

A r m y | N a v y

Chamber's new boss promises toughness

cadets stage Pasadena invasion

City of Pasadena

ONE HUNDRED NORTH GARFIELD AVENUE

PASADENA, CALIFORNIA 91109

LORETTA THOMPSON GLICKMAN
MAYOR
(213) 577-4311

February 6, 1984

Mr. Robert Finch
   and Members of the Army/Navy Foundation
c/o Pasadena Chamber of Commerce
11 West Del Mar Boulevard
Pasadena, California 91101

Dear Bob and Foundation Members,

Although some time has passed since you made history in the City of Pasadena, I feel as I did two months ago when the Army/Navy event took place. For all those people who felt it would not happen, let me assure you that from the day I heard of the plans, I thought it would be an exciting thing for our city.

On behalf of the City, I congratulate you and the Foundation for a job well done. You brought an event to Pasadena with style and in the true character of our city; you brought groups together that have probably never worked so hard to make an event the best we have ever had.

I am personally proud of you and your commitment to Pasadena and I only regret that there are not more people like you.

Sincerely,

Loretta

LORETTA THOMPSON-GLICKMAN
Mayor

LTG:k

PAGE III

Long Beach planning bid
for 1986 Army-Navy Game

SP✺KES

Volume 65   April 6, 1983   Number 39

Traditional Chamber of Commerce lore would have us believe that its chief honchos were universally creatures of brio, gusto and zip, engaged in a kind of Mac Sennett flight of imagination bout with that most seductive of topics — "progress in our town." One could hardly imagine any self respecting Chamber of Commerce admitting to ever having seen better times.

That's the fiction. The fact is that for all too many Chambers, opportunity simply is not recognized because it comes disguised as hard work. Not so in Pasadena. We're lucky; the mood and the realization is 100% upbeat. The Pied Piper of our own Hamlin, Executive V.P. ROLFE ARNHYM has made it so. Ask any of the many Pasadena Rotarians who have volunteered their services under his charismatic spell. They'll tell you that the letter trays on his executive desk read "In, Out and Way-Out." The contents of the "Way-Out" tray are a wonder to behold.

If you enjoy cuddling up to a good mystery, you'll warm to Wednesday's telling.

PASADENA ROTARY PRESENTS

ROLFE W. ARNHYM

"The Army-Navy Game at the Rosebowl—
A Tale of Intrigue and Legerdemain"

Your half hour time investment will make you privy to the wonderment of one of the Chamber's greatest flights of fancy that became reality: bringing the Army-Navy Game extravaganza to our Rosebowl on December 3. The Philadelphia opposition was entrenched; the politics horrendous. Pretty heady stuff. But all that's shooting fish in a barrel compared to the committment to transport, house, feed, chaperon, and foot the bill for the 9,000 men cadet corps of the two academys! The Rapid Deployment Force planning section of the Services may well learn a thing or two from the private sector in jig-time movement of troops.

Pasadena Rotarian Rolfe lives in Claremont. His educational credits include West Point, Command & General Staff College, U.S. Army Management School, and an M.B.A. from George Washington University.

Lt. Colonel Rolfe concluded an eventful career in the army and closeted his copiously decorated jacket to don business pin stripes and start a new career in the civilian world. It started with a deanship with Jones College of Orlando, Florida, and evolved into the role of a management consultant. Thence to the western trek winding up in Pasadena as Program Manager for Electro Optical Systems Division of Xerox in 1975.

An enterprising Chamber of Commerce Board wooed him to the Chamber of Commerce cause and the fast and furious perpetual motion of parades, publicity and progress that constitutes the Chamber's daily fare.

Invocation: BILL SPUCK   Introduction of Visitors & Guests: BOB OLTMAN

Navy sinks Army, 42-13

Army-Navy Group Worked Hard to Make Game Look Easy

Host Some Very Special Guests This Thanksgiving Holiday.

FOOTBALL CLASSIC

November 25, 1983
11:45 AM

Admit One

Disneyland
West Point
Annapolis

Thursday Evening
November 24, 1983
8:00 p.m.–2:00 a.m.

Advance Ticket Sales
$12.00

Disneyland.
WEST POINT
19 83
Annapolis

This portion of the Commemorative
Passport is not valid for admission.

THE UNITED STATES OF AMERICA

TO ALL WHO SHALL SEE THESE PRESENTS, GREETING:

THIS IS TO CERTIFY THAT
THE PRESIDENT OF THE UNITED STATES OF AMERICA
AUTHORIZED BY ACT OF CONGRESS JULY 20, 1942
HAS AWARDED

THE LEGION OF MERIT

TO

LIEUTENANT COLONEL ROLFE G. ARNHYM, ████████, INFANTRY
UNITED STATES ARMY

FOR

EXCEPTIONALLY MERITORIOUS CONDUCT
IN THE PERFORMANCE OF OUTSTANDING SERVICES

IN THE REPUBLIC OF VIETNAM DURING THE PERIOD JUNE 1971 TO MAY 1972

GIVEN UNDER MY HAND IN THE CITY OF WASHINGTON
THIS   27TH   DAY OF   OCTOBER   19 72

FRED C. WEYAND
General, United States Army

SECRETARY OF THE ARMY

By direction of the President, the Legion of Merit

is awarded to

LIEUTENANT COLONEL ROLFE G. ARNHYM, ████████, INFANTRY
UNITED STATES ARMY

who distinguished himself by exceptionally meritorious conduct in the performance of outstanding service during the period June 1971 to May 1972 while serving consecutively as Commanding Officer, 1st Battalion, 6th Infantry Division; Special Assistant for Combat Security to the Commanding General, United States Army Support Command, Cam Ranh Bay; and as a Commander of a United States Army Defense Task Force in the Republic of Vietnam. While acting as brigade commander, he established a joint US/ARVN drug program and initiated combined US/ARVN military operations involving two provinces and two separate ARVN regiments. On 16 August 1971, Lieutenant Colonel Arnhym was assigned as Special Assistant for Combat Security. In this capacity he was responsible for the defense of the Cam Ranh peninsula and the surrounding waters. This responsibility required him to work in close accord with US Army, Navy and Air Force units located on the peninsula and US Army, Republic of Korea Army and Republic of Vietnam forces on the mainland. Upon his arrival, he initiated a program of updating all defense plans and upgrading the defenses of the different installations. On 10 January 1972 the US Army Defense Task Force, Cam Ranh Bay (Provisional) was formed with Lieutenant Colonel Arnhym commanding. The task force became responsible for the security and defense of the remaining US key facilities at Cam Ranh Bay. Lieutenant Colonel Arnhym's professional competence and outstanding achievements are in keeping with the highest traditions of the military service and reflect great credit upon himself, this Command and the United States Army.

Appendix Page I
- 1983 Army-Navy Foundation Official Program (Cover Image)

Appendix Page II
- www.rolfegarnhym.com for full articles.

Appendix Page III
- Thompson-Glickman, Loretta. Letter to author. 6 Feb 1984. TS.

Appendix Page IV
- "Pasa-Beach Pressed News" Pasadena Chamber of Commerce Commemorative Program for Retirement of Rolfe G. Arnhym. 13 May 1985.

Appendix Page V
- Pasadena Chamber of Commerce. "Pasadena Rotary Presents Rolfe W. Arnhym." *Spokes* [Pasadena, CA] 6 Apr 1983. Print.

Appendix Page VI - VII
- www.rolfegarnhym.com for full articles.

Appendix Page VIII
- "The Legion of Merit" awarded to Lt. Colonel Rolfe G. Arnhym of the United States Army Infantry. Awarded 27 Oct 1983.

Appendix Page IX
- Photograph of the Color Guard at The United States Military Academy (West Point)

Appendix Page X - XIV
- Photos by Ryan Gautier